Praise for The Job Sear

If there is a job search in your future, then the **JOB SEARCH** *Manifesto* should be as well. Great skills won't matter if you can't get in front of the decision-makers, and with so much competition in the market, why leave things up to chance?

"This book thoroughly covers all the steps in a job search with insider tips, advice and examples from two of the leading experts in the industry. Take the guess work out of your next job search with "***The* JOB SEARCH *Manifesto***" – you'll be glad you did."

Dawn Graham, PhD, *Author of "Switchers: How Smart Professionals Change Careers and Seize Success"*

"Whether you're just starting your job search or need a jumpstart, ***The* JOB SEARCH *Manifesto*** reveals the hidden secrets to marketing yourself like a pro. It's like having your own personal career coach in your pocket."

Robert Carroll: *Career and Leadership Coach | Former Technology Executive*

"***The* JOB SEARCH *Manifesto*** should be required reading for everyone in today's job market. Its emphasis on the life-long development and use of modern job search skills is one of its key strengths and is a clear reminder that we should always be preparing for our next move. What I found to be especially valuable was the emphasis on building a brand, one that instills confidence and clarity, and that can be woven into all aspects of the job search.

I also appreciate how the authors delineated the importance of networking and how the nurturing of career-long relationships is key to conducting an effective job search. "

Mark Guterman, *Career and Executive Coach, Author of "Common Sense for Uncommon Times: The Power of Balance in Work, Family, and Personal Life,"*

the JOB SEARCH *manifesto*

By Steve Hernandez
and Mike Manoske

Crystal Cove Media
Hayward, California

The Job Search Manifesto | Steve Hernandez and Mike Manoske.

First edition.

ISBN: 978-1-7370180-3-2 eBook

ISBN: 978-1-7370180-2-5 Paperback

Book Design by Yayun Chang Cahill dimsumlove.com

Contents

Introduction

We've seen it, felt it, and heard it hundreds of times. As recruiters, we've heard it in the voices of the candidates we've worked with: they talk about a job they really want, but they don't understand the process they need to use to acquire the position.

We see it in the faces of students or clients who want to change their career direction but are afraid to take even a first step.

We've felt it from those who didn't see the layoff coming and were blindsided.

What we experience is people dealing with fear, uncertainly, and doubt (FUD) about their career direction—and most immediately about their job search. In many cases, FUD triggers avoidance, where people just don't take action. It locks them up; their unhappiness in their current role is less daunting than the fear of navigating change.

Job Change Is Inevitable

Yet the reality is that job change is inevitable. Here's proof based on data from the US Bureau of Labor Statistics and our over three decades of recruiting and career coaching.

A twenty-five-year-old who works until sixty-five will change jobs every 4.2 years, talk with at least four organizations or more for each job change, and interview with five people (or more) for each job posting they apply for.

This twenty-five-year-old will change jobs ten times in their career, which involves (1):

- interviewing with forty companies or more
- individually interviewing with two hundred people or more
- updating their LinkedIn profile forty times annually, and
- updating, enhancing, or restructuring their résumé more than forty times, if done for each role.

The numbers are daunting, even though we were conservative in our estimates. In Silicon Valley, the average tenure is 3.5 years (2), and in certain roles and companies the time is even shorter. The interview numbers come from our experience as recruiters. A typical interview cycle consists of three rounds and involves at least five people: a recruiter, a hiring manager, and three staff members. (3) There's good news if you are over twenty-five or plan to retire earlier: you have fewer job searches ahead. But the stress and headache will stay the same if you continue to follow the same tired process.

Is This You?

You're probably ready for change if any or most of these situations exist for you:

- your job is unrewarding or boring, or, worse, you've been laid off
- your pay is stagnant or even declining
- there are no advancement opportunities in your current job
- the economy has you deeply concerned about your job and income security
- you work for a company and leadership that you don't respect, or you work on a team that is toxic, and/or
- you want to make a major change in your life—get married, move, buy a home, or go back to school—but your job doesn't offer the flexibility or income to do it.

If these situations resonate with you, then they will likely trigger you to slowly begin a job search. If you haven't done a job search in a number of years, then you're likely to follow a dated, tired model—one that is slow, frustrating, and demoralizing.

The Old, Broken Approach

This is a lot of work to leave to chance, using a hit-or-miss process. Yet many people treat job searches and career changes as a necessary evil, like going to the DMV to renew their license.

So you begin a job search and follow the familiar, well-worn steps. You:

- update your résumé (the same one you've used for years)
- find jobs and apply online by sending in the updated résumé
- wait
- react to any incoming reply and hopefully make it through the interview process
- nervously negotiate your next salary, feeling powerless and wondering how much you left on the table, and
- hope the next job is better than the last.

Or there's potentially an even sadder situation: you stay in a job because you fear the job search process. The above mentioned outmoded job search method is the "standard model," and it's no wonder people dread changing jobs. This reactive, one-size-fits-all approach leaves you powerless each time you want to change your job or career direction.

The bottom line is that if you don't have a coherent and efficient plan, an effective brand, and a decent network or network-building plan, then changing jobs will be a repetitively painful exercise.

Addressing the Challenge

We've made it our mission (and our careers) to share the best practices of a job search and career transition to give more control back to the candidate. It was because of this desire to give more power to job searchers that Steve developed the Job Search Action Group (JSAG) program at Wharton's Executive MBA Program in San Francisco, where he is the director of career advancement.

JSAG is a seven-session, fourteen-week program that breaks down the job search into a series of easily accomplished steps that build on one another. Steve created the program and invited Mike to collaborate. Since then we have trained hundreds of students in job search best practices while refining the job search steps and methods.

Though we are unable to share the data directly, the results have been consistent and solid: we see more than half the students change roles while in JSAG. Additionally, more than 80 percent have changed roles within a year of graduation.

What makes these numbers even more impressive is that this is an executive MBA program; students are working full-time while taking a rigorous set of classes. Moreover, students who join JSAG are executing a job search at the same time! To accommodate their schedule, we often lead sessions at seven thirty on Saturday mornings.

In the last year, this has been even more challenging with COVID-19 and lockdown, as the program has been completely remote.

Using the JOB SEARCH *Manifesto* in *Boot Camps*

We expanded our outreach and began leading abridged versions of our programs in Job Search Boot Camps. We did this in conjunction with HireClub (http://hireclub.com). They have a thriving Facebook community and are also on Clubhouse.

The results were the same: we saw participants gain confidence in their job search and many landed new roles, even in the midst of the pandemic.

Who We Are

The program we've developed comes from our unique vantage points: almost thirty years combined as recruiters, both inside and external to companies. Then add more than two decades as career coaches, both in the academic environment at Wharton and in a private career-coaching practice.

Prior to Wharton, Steve was an executive recruiter for almost a decade, retained by successful organizations to discover and recruit top leadership talent in every area of their organizations. During that time Steve also completed a master's degree in psychology. He has been director of career advancement for Wharton's Executive MBA Program in San Francisco since 2011.

Mike was a manager in both health care and technology who transitioned into recruiting leadership more than two decades ago. He has been both an executive recruiter and an in-house recruiting leader. Mike is a graduate of the Hudson Institute of

Coaching and is a certified coach with the International Coaching Federation.

The program has been used outside academia, both in private practice and in "boot camps," which are shortened versions of the program for a Job Search Community HireClub.

We've seen the program work for job seekers in all skills areas and at all experience levels. We have also found that documenting our program sped up job seekers' processes, so several years ago, we began to collate our many slide decks and exercises. The result is this book: *The Job Search Manifesto*.

the JOB SEARCH Manifesto

The goal of this book is to provide good news and encouragement: you can have more control over your job search process and the outcome. *The Job Search Manifesto* is robust and has been field tested for job searches and career transitions. You can use these steps now and throughout your career.

The program covers every component of your job search from getting started to negotiation and all the steps in between.

Our job search work and *The Job Search Manifesto* approach worked before the COVID-19 pandemic and continues to help clients and students during this challenging time. In fact, we'll highlight places where the book's best practices have worked even better in these conditions.

Because of the consistency of job changes and the need for job search strategy recalibration, we will continually update this book.

Why a *Manifesto*?

We'd been circulating early drafts of this book to program participants and private clients for several years. One student read the draft, came into Steve's office, and enthusiastically said, "This is really your manifesto." It made perfect sense and gave us our title.

Dictionary.com defines a manifesto as a "a public declaration of intentions, opinions, objectives, or motives" (4). *The Job Search Manifesto* has all of this: strong intentions along with fact-based opinions and objectives. Our motive and passion drive all of this, which leads to the first principle of the book: *Job searching is a skill set that gets stronger, deeper, and richer throughout your career.*

That is the core of *The Job Search Manifesto*. We have other strong principles that anchor this book, listed in the next section at the beginning of each chapter. These principles are the guideposts for the work that's done in each chapter and throughout the book.

How to Use This Book

The Job Search Manifesto has a road map you can follow with exercises that will help you prepare for each step. The process is meant to build on the work you do from each prior step of the chapter, although this does not mean you have to work progressively from Step One through Step Eight.

Each job search is different, and each stage in your career is different. You may already be actively interviewing as you read this book. Even better, you might be already negotiating an offer. If so, congratulations! The chapters on interviewing and negotiations can help you immediately.

Remember, our core principle is that job searching is a skill that needs to be developed. Building a strong brand statement and a solid LinkedIn profile, and creating long-lasting, mutually beneficial business relationships, require effort throughout your working life, not just during a job search.

We recommend you start at the beginning if you are just embarking on a job search or even just contemplating one. You don't have to take on the entire job search at once. *The Job Search Manifesto* is designed to give you small, quick wins that will help you create a direction and better articulate your skills and potential impact in your next role.

The section after this introduction includes the principles that set the tone for this book. They'll give you a sense of our direction and approach. The principles specific to each step are shown again at the top of the chapter for each step.

After you've reviewed the principles, you'll see the process steps to follow in *The Job Search Manifesto*. You may notice that the order is different from most job search approaches. We believe you must have a clear idea of the roles you are targeting and how you bring value (your brand statement). Without clear targets and a solid brand statement, your progress forward will be slow and awkward.

Don't try to complete all the steps at once. Take your time with the work for each step. Trying to do the entire process in a couple of days defeats the purpose. Remember, you are building a skill, not slogging through a frustrating, rare transition. Also, don't stop moving ahead if one step seems challenging. You don't have to be perfect, especially when you're just starting out. It's better to get some work done and move ahead. Remember, there is no "perfect," just continued growth.

We also know that job searching is often a roller coaster, especially as you first implement *The Job Search Manifesto* tools and approaches. That's why building a series of small wins is important.

Each chapter also contains a true story about someone we've worked with who followed *The Job Search Manifesto* and had success. We share these anecdotes to help you see that many people have been in the place you're in now and have succeeded in taking the next steps in their careers.

Don't Isolate; Find Support

Equally important to working through the sections of the book and creating small wins is being aware of the potential for isolation. Searching for a job, especially if you are not working, can be lonely and can lead to depression, especially during a pandemic.

JSAG, which Steve founded at Wharton, is built around the content you'll see in this book, along with mutual assistance and support. Each class has their own JSAG WhatsApp group, and they are all still active today, years after they graduated. Participants still share their wins, losses, ideas, and job leads. They continue to support and encourage one another. We've seen the same with the boot camps we've led outside of Wharton.

There are many social media–based job search communities; others are sponsored by nonprofits and local communities. Some, like HireClub, are broad and welcome all. Others are more specific, such as parents or caregivers returning to work, or industry-specific groups focused on marketing or finance and accounting, for example. Audition several and see what feels supportive and helpful.

Keep in mind that friends and family, though well meaning, often give less than helpful advice and guidance. They don't do it maliciously; they usually don't have a current view of the marketplace or your specific industry. Let them know you appreciate their support and that you are following current best practices in your job search.

the **JOB SEARCH** *road map*

We've broken down a job search into nine manageable action areas. You don't have to be an expert at each one, nor do you have to start at Targeting. We'll make a case Each step reinforces the others and gives you more and more strength and confidence as you move forward. Here's the road map and a synopsis of each step.that following this process has proven to consistently work.

1. **Targeting**—identify industries, companies, and roles based on your current interests, passions, relevant skills, and experience.

2. **Brand**—build a compelling brand statement (not an elevator pitch) that you will use throughout your job search and beyond. You'll quickly see how important your brand statement is and the number of places it will be used in varied delivery formats.

3. **Relationship building**—create, grow, and maintain a relationship-building/networking model for your current job search. Develop a strong reach-out message and share it with your target connections.

4. **Sourcing**—identify job opportunities using multiple resources.

5. **LinkedIn**—create and update a compelling LinkedIn profile from the content and information you've developed toward your target audience. You'll tie your brand, work history, key accomplishments, and skills to your aspirational career function.

6. **Résumé**—update your résumé and treat it as a marketing document, not your life story.

7. **Application tactics**—apply best practices on how to develop and manage "multiple paths" of job applications.

8. **Interviewing**—learn to tell your story strongly and effectively during informal and formal interviews.

9. **Negotiation**—learn the "levers": methods and effective communication to use during negotiations.

Too often we've seen people begin a job search by just updating their résumés. It's one of those challenging moments for us as career coaches because that's not where people should begin their job search.

A job search should begin by having clearly defined interests, marketable skills and experience, and targets. Once you know the industries, companies, and roles you seek, build a compelling brand statement aimed at solving their problems. Updating a résumé before you've identified the audience and their needs is a waste of your time.

With a clear focus and a good branding statement, relationship building becomes far easier. A compelling brand is at the core of your job search and career success.

It surprises people that we prioritize LinkedIn before updating a résumé, but that comes from our recruiting background. Your LinkedIn profile is essentially a one-page website about you. It's specifically designed for recruiters and leaders to find you and understand you. A well-written LinkedIn profile that speaks clearly to your areas of interest and expertise will help recruiters and others find you.

With a solid brand statement and a clear LinkedIn profile, your résumé becomes much easier to write. We'll discuss simple résumé models in the coming chapters.

We often assist clients with "white-knuckle" feelings about interviewing. We'll spend a good amount of time sharing models and simple approaches to get the blood flowing back to your knuckles. One of our missions with both candidates and companies is to shift the interview process into meaningful conversations. We'll go into more detail on storytelling within the résumé section.

Finally, we want to help you establish a mindset and strategy for negotiations that will gets results. As recruiters who've extended hundreds and hundreds of offers, we'll discuss how to understand each lever or component of an offer and the negotiating techniques involved in each one.

Yes, there are a multiple steps to follow, but don't be intimidated. We've structured this so you can move as quickly or as slowly as you'd like, while seeing progress at each point along the way.

How This Book Is Structured

Each chapter begins with a "manifesto": several bullet points we believe are important to keep in mind. A real-world story from our clients follows (we have changed names and other identifiers for confidentiality purposes).

Each chapter contains exercises and work that build on previous chapters. The work you'll do will be immediately beneficial to your job search.

You'll do some writing; to make that easier, a reference section at the end has word lists and other resources for you. Use them liberally.

the Job Search Manifesto Strategy

In an active job search, you'll be reaching out to multiple audiences, including hiring managers and advocates in organizations you're interested in. This is a change from the typical job search approach. Historically, job searching has meant sending out résumés and waiting for responses. Yes, you will still do a bit of that, but in a much more strategic and measured way.

You've all seen and heard about the "hidden job market." It is real, but understanding the background and best practices on tapping into it is the foundation to *The Job Search Manifesto* program.

SUMMARY

- *The Job Search Manifesto* is designed to get you the next job in your career but also to develop the skills to make better and stronger steps throughout your career.
- With ever-shrinking job durations, job searching needs to become a skill, not an activity to be avoided until the last minute.
- There are nine steps to a job search, and we'll show you the best practices for each.
- Build a support system; don't isolate. Job searching can be lonely. Look for friends, colleagues, or even groups online.
- If you are reading this during an active job search, you can skip to the chapters that relate to the job search stage you're currently in, especially if you're actively interviewing or are even in negotiations.

Let's get started!

TARGETING

Manifesto

- Targeting is equal parts self-assessment and detective work.
- Targeting eliminates the “leave first, plan later” career approach.
- Building a profile of your next role will lead to an action plan that’s very likely to succeed.

Sarah Improved Her Aim

Sarah was at a crossroads in her career. She had moved up the ranks in marketing at a large enterprise software company, but after a management change, she ran into political challenges she felt she couldn't overcome. Out of frustration, Sarah abruptly resigned.

The relief she felt was brief, quickly replaced with fear and worry. Sarah had bailed without a plan of action. She regrouped and began a job search that followed the "old model" and identified a couple of likely landing spots. In only a few months, Sarah was back in a marketing leadership role at another software company.

Unfortunately, she hadn't done much research and knew only that the company had a "good reputation" and was profitable. Her tenure there was more of the same. Sarah didn't feel connected to the leadership team or the company culture. She left after a year and decided to take a hard look at her career direction; she started career coaching.

The coaching work began targeting by starting at the top: What kind of industries did she want to work in? Her career had always been based inside software companies with complex products. Much of her marketing career had been customer focused, and that was her sweet spot.

Her targeting work expanded her choices. Sarah wanted to stay in software and began to look at consumer product roles, but she also looked at software consulting firms and resellers. After doing the research, she realized that resellers had solid financials and a more targeted customer base. Sarah could work in a smaller arena with deeper customer contact.

The list of companies in this space narrowed to a couple, and Sarah interviewed well. She had done her homework on both the challenges and opportunities these companies faced. Her background in larger firms was helpful and gave her an impressive understanding of the customer community and competitive landscape.

Sarah also looked at culture and changed her approach to include "interviewing the interviewers," especially her potential bosses and the leadership team. Her coaching emphasized being an equal partner in the interview process and assessing the culture. The company she eventually selected met much of her targeting criteria. It was financially strong but innovative and customer focused.

She clicked with the leadership team, especially her boss. Even when a political challenge came up early on, she and her boss quickly worked through it.

Sarah developed new skills that helped her find a good place to grow, and the assessment skills she developed related to evaluating the type of organizations and roles available will help her use strong career decision-making next time she changes roles.

About This Chapter

That feeling of frustration in a job is universal; internal and external situations are constantly changing. Also universal are the daydreams to leave and start a cool new chapter in our lives. But as Sarah discovered, without a clear target or aspiration and a realistic action plan, leaving is often worse than staying.

Creating a target or profile for your job search helps to keep the emotions down and enthusiasm high. It's not enough to know an organization has great products or is profitable; targeting goes deeper. You need to understand the company's direction, culture, and, most of all, how your skills and experiences would fit.

Mapping your skills and experiences to your target opportunities requires both curiosity and honesty. It's easy to rattle off your strengths for a job. But knowing your weaknesses or growth areas is equally important. This chapter will walk you through a simple process to "prime the pump" on your next opportunities and direction. We will start at a high level, and then you'll inventory your current strengths and readiness.

Don't expect to do this chapter in a single session. Step away and come back to it. The goal is to go from fuzzy ideas to a clearer idea, and that can take time.

Areas of Interest

We've broken down job interest areas into three broad categories: *industries*, *organizations*, and *roles*.

Industries can be wide (such as nonprofit, academic) or more specific (financial services, consumer electronics, or tech). It's also OK to have several interest areas.*Organizations* are more specific; here's where you name names. You could list Amazon, Genentech, 3M, or several start-ups that intrigue you.

Roles are more granular and detailed. Typically, here you'd list job titles, and that's fine. But consider going a little deeper by listing what you'd *like* to be doing. These could be:

- owning marketing strategy for a product line
- having P&L (profit and loss) responsibility for a business unit
- being the sales leader for a small business SaaS (software-as-a-service) product.

EXERCISE: LIST YOUR AREAS OF INTEREST

List your interests in each of the three categories. Be open and stretch your ideas a little bit.

Nothing is out of bounds in this exercise— *dream a little bit!*

Industries	
Organizations	

Roles	

EXERCISE: Rank Your Top Three Targets

Now that you have several targets, let's focus on the top three, no matter the category. Write them down below.

RANK	TARGET
1	
2	
3	

Evaluate the Targets—And Your Readiness

We're using a marketing modeling approach called "personas," and we want you to create a persona for your interest targets. It's no problem if you have only one or two. The goal is to build a comprehensive picture to prepare you for further action steps.

TARGET INFORMATION CATEGORIES	YOUR READINESS CATEGORIES
• Target's important facts and figures • Target's goals and aspirations • Target's challenges	• Why are you a good fit today? • What are your current gaps?

A persona in the context of marketing refers to the ideal customer for your business. Personas are defined by a mixture of attributes. (6)
The readiness exercise builds a persona by looking at five categories: three are based on your current knowledge about the target, and the other two focus on your readiness.

Your Target's Brand

A key to this exercise is the brand or popularity of your target. The premise behind this idea is that the better known your target, the more job competition you will face. This means the more popular the company, the more knowledge and preparation you need.

An easy way to think about a brand is the larger or more popular it is, the more competition. The greater the competition, the more you need to prepare. We are not asking you to do deep prep work now—an overview is fine. But we do want you to keep in mind that the job search prep work will be higher with larger brands.

Brands can also apply to roles. Currently we see lots of interest in product management. Knowing this, a candidate can build the persona or profile of a successful product manager.

There are three brand levels: small, medium, and large. A few examples are shown below.

SMALL BRANDS

INDUSTRY: can be an emerging business category or an industry that is static or even declining.

COMPANY: usually start-ups or small firms. They have minimal press, and their products or services are either in development or they're in a small niche market. A small brand target might serve a small region or have a small range of products or services.

ROLE: much like the industry, these are roles that are new and still being defined or long-time roles that are stable or being phased out.

EXAMPLES: start-ups with either angel funding or a round of funding, possibly in "stealth" mode, or family-owned businesses. Examples include Afresh Technologies and solo.io.

MEDIUM BRANDS

INDUSTRY: they have a product or service they recently brought to market that may be competing with a larger player in the industry space.

COMPANY: there is press and publicity you can easily uncover. Often you can learn a lot from the background, business philosophy, and approach you learn about from the founders. There may also be some initial feedback on Glassdoor, but this is likely minimal. Also look at recent leadership team hires to see which other people are joining.

ROLE: should be clearer than in a small brand, with a nice range of responsibility and influence. Advancement may not be as clear, so defining that is important.

EXAMPLES: they have had a product in the marketplace for one to two years or have released a significant new product or service in the same time line. Examples include Sonder and HashiCorp.

LARGE BRANDS

INDUSTRY: a long-entrenched market leader.

COMPANY: they are well known, if not a household name. A key thing to research: are they still "out in front" or fighting more competitors, especially disrupters in their space?

ROLE: should be well defined with career growth paths available. The trade-off might be a smaller portfolio of responsibility and more levels involved in decision-making.

EXAMPLES: IPO or soon to IPO; can also be private by choice. Examples include Facebook, Google, and Goldman Sachs.

EXERCISE: BUILD THE PERSONA OF YOUR TOP THREE TARGETS

With your top targets identified and an understanding of the five attributes along with brand size for each target, you'll build a persona for your top three targets.

Start with the first one, and take your time. This is not a timed exercise, and it will take you some time. You'll learn how to do research along with assessing your own skill, which will take time and patience. But the ability to build these profiles and the insights you receive from doing so will pay off, big time.

Target #1: ....

Brand size: ....

YOUR CURRENT KNOWLEDGE	COMMENTS AND DETAILS
Target's important facts and figures	
Target's goals and aspirations	
Target's challenges	
Why are you a good fit today?	
Your current gaps	

Target #2: ....

Brand size: ....

YOUR CURRENT KNOWLEDGE	COMMENTS AND DETAILS
Target's important facts and figures	
Target's goals and aspirations	
Target's challenges	
Why are you a good fit today?	
Your current gaps	

Target #3: ....

Brand size: ....

YOUR CURRENT KNOWLEDGE	COMMENTS AND DETAILS
Target's important facts and figures	
Target's goals and aspirations	
Target's challenges	
Why are you a good fit today?	
Your current gaps	

Summary

It's exciting to meld your career aspirations with research. Targeting is the place where you ground dreams with research. The biggest task in this part of your job search is investing time to validate your targets.

- The key question in this chapter is this: How well do your targets align with your transferrable skills, relevant experience, interests, network, and long-term career aspirations?

- Become an expert in your target spaces. Know the players, market data, industry nuances, leaders in the space, and the backgrounds and experience of people in your target roles.

- Be clear on the value proposition you'll offer to your targets.

- Look at your skills and experience gaps. Once you know what you need to build and add to your skills and experience, you can create and execute an action plan to fill the gaps.

The following chapters will help you fill those gaps and make you a strong candidate for your targets.

YOUR BRAND STATEMENT

Manifesto

- Your brand statement is the foundation of your communication in every part of your job search.
- Your brand statement is the answer to the question, "Tell me about yourself."
- Brand statements directly explain how your skills and experiences can help an organization.

Catalina's Bold Transition

Catalina was looking to make a big change in her career, and it all hinged on better describing herself. She was a successful sales account manager in the consumer products space and was finishing her MBA. Initially, Catalina planned to move into a sales leadership role, but marketing classes really excited her. So halfway through the program, she changed direction and decided to fully pursue roles in marketing.

Making this change had an immediate ripple effect on her current company; they didn't encourage the transition. So Catalina knew she would have to look for another organization. That meant that describing herself through her brand statement was even more important.

The challenge she worked on through coaching was to make a strong case for a marketing role without having direct, hands-on marketing experience. She went after this head-on by opening her brand statement with this simple, powerful phrase: "salesperson turned marketer."

This phrase in her brand statement didn't waffle or equivocate; Catalina was stating clearly that she was a marketer with a sales background. She added her successes in customer obsession and understanding. Catalina also included her skills (gained from business school) in analytics and leadership.

Being clear about marketing was important in her job search because she had no marketing roles in her experience. Her brand statement in both her LinkedIn profile and her résumé helped recruiters and others to have a clear understanding of Catalina's direction and the immediate value she offered.

A large consumer products company saw this and understood her. They are a very traditional organization but saw the value of including Catalina's frontline sales experience in their marketing group. Her interviews went smoothly, and she was offered a role in product marketing. She jumped at the opportunity, even though it was a small step down. But it gave her the chance to get solid marketing experience, which she has continued to build on.

Without that strong, affirmative statement, Catalina's job search could well have taken much longer. The clarity in her brand statement smoothed out and sped up her job search and career transition.

About This Chapter

Elevator pitches, career summaries, background stories, bios—there are way too many terms for the foundation of your job search and your career planning. It needs to be a permanent part of your career planning, not just something to occasionally revisit. We call it your brand statement, and getting it comfortable and right for you is key.

Your brand statement is at the heart of a job search and career success. You'll use versions of it in your LinkedIn profile, résumé, and future interviews.

We want to emphasize that this is *not* bragging; it's much more important than that. Bragging is making statements blindly and only to make yourself appear great. Brand statements are not bragging; they are concise statements meant to trigger additional dialogues and conversation.

Your brand statement consists of your skills, strengths, and accomplishments, which are based on your talent, passions, education, and experience. It's a concise statement that triggers interest in learning more about you. Psychologist and executive coach Anna Ranieri describes it this way:

> You tell your story in a way that connects the dots . . . You must [ensure] that your audience can identify the thread that runs through your career narrative and make sense of your varied skills, training, experiences, and choices.
>
> First, if others are ever going to understand your trajectory, you must make sense of it yourself. Identify the themes that run through your professional life. (6)

The purpose of a brand statement is to connect the dots in your experiences to clearly show the value you bring to an organization.

When writing their brand statements, many people fall into the trap of simply reciting their résumé. Your brand statement should not be a summary of your résumé. Instead, you should think of it as a brief explanation of your career journey that answers two key questions:

- What experiences and accomplishments are the foundations of your career?

- How do those experiences and accomplishments bring value to organizations?

To create a powerful and resilient brand statement, we've broken it down into three components: *successes*, *domain experience*, and *career superpowers*.

We'll take a detailed look at each of these areas of your career to date, listing out key elements for each. Once done, we'll integrate each area with a summary. That summary is your brand statement.

Successes

Successes and accomplishments are typically easy to list. They're the wins you've had throughout your career and life. For this step we'll go broad and then focus more narrowly as we close in on your brand statement.

To help you think broadly, we have four areas in which to think about your accomplishments: *academic*, *early career*, *current career*, and *personal*.

Academic success examples include:

- membership or leadership of a student group
- participation in a study abroad program
- internships
- published academic research and presentation at significant forums

Early career success examples include:

- being a key team member who brought a new product or service to market
- working closely with a key client or clients where the work contributed a lot to the bottom line

Current career success examples include:

- how your leadership roles have grown over the course of your career
- how projects you've led have had high impact
- how systems and processes you've developed have created a strong benefit to the organization

Personal success examples include:

- team or personal sports achievements
- hobbies or personal interests that received awards or other recognition
- nonprofit or community work in which you've been involved

EXERCISE: WRITE OUT YOUR SUCCESSES

Looking at your work history, take a long view and go back as far as your academic experience. If you are just starting out, don't feel intimidated if you only have a few years of work experience and can't fill out each section. It's more important to capture the successes.

Using the examples above, write down your successes. In each phase of your career journey, detail how your responsibilities grew from the start of that phase until you moved to the next phase.

	SUCCESSES
Academic	
Early career	
Current career	
Personal	

Career Superpowers

The concept of a superpower may sound trite and overused, but when it comes to a brand statement, it's the perfect metaphor. How you deliver a task or solution is a superpower. There are two elements.

In his breakthrough book *Finding Flow: The Psychology of Engagement with Everyday Life*, psychologist Mihaly Csikszentmihalyi describes that sweet spot in performance: "People tend to use their mind and body to its fullest, and consequently feel that what they do is important, and feel good about themselves while doing it." (7)

That feeling of performing at a high level, feeling relaxed, and being fully engaged is the first element of career superpowers. It's a strength or a skill, but that's all it is.

The second element is what turns skills or strengths into superpowers: articulating the value the skills bring to the company, team, or organization.

It's easy to say, "I connect well with people, and I fully engage with them as we talk." But that's not a career superpower: that's just a skill. It's a description of what puts you in a state of "flow," but it doesn't explain how the ability to connect with others benefits the organization.

When you add in the second element, the benefit to the organization, this is how that superpower would be described:

> "I'm a project manager who fully engages with teams across my organization to make them feel connected and empowered."

To summarize, a career superpower consists of two elements:

- a skill that's performed at a high level—and the person is fully engaged as they do it
- the clearly stated values these skills contribute to an organization

When you put these elements together, you are explaining your career superpowers. Below are a few career superpower examples:

- My team and I take whiteboard ideas and turn them into market-ready products.

The skills in this example are related to project management. They turn into career superpowers when the value (moving through a full product development cycle) is explained:

- A strong ability to listen and understand helps me give my customers the best solutions for their needs.

Strong listening is the skill. When this listening skill is applied to a sales, customer service, or customer success role, the value comes through. That makes it a career superpower.

- My hands-on engineering skills allows me to identify and implement key features that solve challenging technical issues.

- My deep understanding of finance processes and best practices gives my company faster and more accurate reporting and analysis.

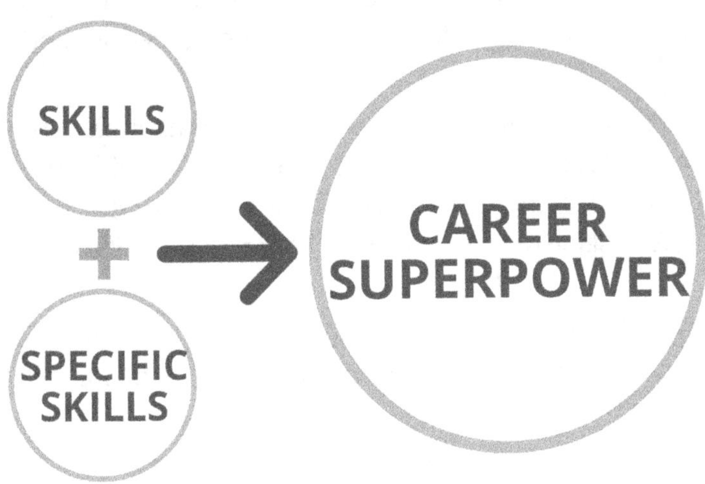

Capturing Your Skills—Hard and Soft

We break down the listing of your skills into a couple of areas. Completing written self-descriptions can be challenging, so breaking them down into sections makes them a lot less daunting. But as described in this chapter, describing your skills is essential to your job search and job success.

The best way to focus on your skills is to look at the two groups of skills: hard and soft. Hard skills and soft skills are phrases that are always tossed around in job searches and career development, but let's make them clear.

Hard skills are tangible, measurable skills usually gained through a combination of formal education, training, and experience. When an organization wants to "test skills," they are testing a candidate's hard skills.

Soft skills are qualitative, hard to measure, but more important than hard skills, according to a survey by LinkedIn Learning:

> Let's start with the skills all professionals should learn, regardless of what they do. These are "soft" skills, although in practice they are anything but: 57 percent of leaders say soft skills are more important than hard skills. (8)

When making a skills list, consider both your hard and soft skills and how they have factored into your accomplishments.

Below are some hard and soft skills examples.

HARD SKILLS	SOFT SKILLS
Accounting	Communication
Sales	Leadership
Website design	Time management
Engineering	Creativity
Carpentry	Negotiation
Project/product or program management	Conflict management
Data analysis	Empathy
Writing—both technical and business	Team building

We've found it helpful for people to write their skills by looking holistically at their lives. Often people forget to look at skills they've gained academically and skills they've acquired in their personal lives.

Academically, you may have led a team project that produced some interesting research or looked at a problem in a unique way. The skills you develop there might include research, data analysis, and technical writing. Soft skills might include collaboration, communication, and perhaps even public speaking.

In your personal life, being on the board of a nonprofit or homeowners association is also invaluable experience. Doing so has probably developed your skills in financial analysis, budgeting, and negotiation. Don't forget hobbies and personal-interest areas either. If you're hands-on in repair carpentry or even a craft, think about the skills developed from these activities.

Your career is the most obvious place to look, but make sure to examine your career in total. This is especially true if you've made significant changes in the direction of your career. Course skills you gain in one industry can have value in others. We've coached people who moved from health care to technology because they had strong analytical and data-analysis skills plus solid leadership experience. Those combinations of hard and soft skills are almost always transferable.

Specific Values

As we said at the beginning of the chapter, skills are terrific, but they don't become superpowers unless you explain the specific value those skills bring to the next organization or role you're seeking. It's critical to your job search and career advancement that you can articulate these specific values. But why are we emphasizing the word *specific*?

This is where your targeting research meets your branding statement. You must clearly state the values that come with your skills that directly apply to that role, organization, or industry. The more specific, the better. Don't depend on the reader of your LinkedIn profile or résumé to connect those dots—that's your job. When you connect your skills to the specific value they bring, you've explained your superpowers.

The following exercises will help you craft a clear and compelling brand statement that can be easily updated as your career progresses. Having a good brand statement will make your job search a lot easier, which should in turn make you more confident going forward.

Look at each of the three categories, think about ways you've succeeded in each of them, and write them below.

Skill: Ability to quickly synthesize information.

Specific value: I help my organizations make decisions and take meaningful action faster.

Skill: A deep understanding of financial modeling in the consumer product industry.

Specific value: The financial risks and rewards are well understood before we enter the market.

Skill: A hands-on expert in search engine marketing.

Specific value: I increase product sales or customer acquisition through cost-effective online marketing programs.

Skill: Ability to roadmap a product from ideation to delivery.

Specific value: I can often spot project or product issues early and get them resolved before they affect delivery dates.

EXERCISE: List Your Skills and Specific Values

In the table below, write down skills and specific values in the various parts of your education and career. Don't worry if your career is short, just capture your skills and values.

	SKILLS	SPECIFIC VALUE
Academic		
Career		
Personal		

Building Your Career Superpower

With the last exercise completed, the next step—to turn these into a superpower—is simple: combine the skill with the specific value. Here are the previous examples, now transformed into career superpowers.

Skill: Ability to quickly synthesize information.

Specific value: I help my organizations make decisions and take meaningful action faster.

Superpower: I help my organization make better and more meaningful decisions by quickly synthesizing critical information.

Skill: A deep understanding of financial modeling in the consumer product industry.

Specific value: The financial risks and rewards are well understood before we enter the market.

Superpower: I create detailed financial models that clearly articulate risks and rewards before we bring a new product to market.

Skill: A hands-on expert in search engine marketing.

Specific value: I increase product sales or customer acquisition through cost-effective online marketing programs.

Superpower: With my expertise in search engine marketing, I create cost-effective online marketing programs that increase sales and customer acquisition.

Skill: Ability to roadmap a product from ideation to delivery.

Specific value: I can often spot project or product issues early and get them resolved before they affect delivery dates.

Superpower: With my experience in bringing multiple products from idea to the marketplace, I can spot challenges early, helping to keep us on track.

EXERCISE: WRITE YOUR CAREER SUPERPOWERS

Use the examples and craft your own career superpowers. Combine the skills and the specific values together and see how it sounds. Remember, this is a place to practice, so give yourself plenty of time to edit. We've left spaces for you to list several superpowers if that feels right to you.

SKILL AND SPECIFIC VALUE	SUPERPOWER

Domain Experience

Domain experience is another element in explaining your expertise. We use domain experience as a way of clarifying that yours fits well into the industries, companies, and roles you are considering. Colleague and friend Dr. Dawn Graham explains domain experience in her book *Switchers: How Smart Professionals Change Careers—and Seize Success*. She uses the word *expertise*, but it's the same as domain experience:

> Your expertise isn't just a list of competencies like "problem solving" or "managing teams." You can begin with these broad terms, but you'll need to go much deeper than the list of words you might find in a job description. It's not enough to tell them you have a skill. (9)

Domain experience is the result of aggregating or bundling your skills together. What do your accomplishments and your career superpowers look like when you assess them in total? The following example takes the accomplishments, skills, values, and superpowers and creates a concise summary. Notice its brevity.

Domain experience examples include accounting systems, *analytics tools*, and *management reporting*.

The domain experience comes from the accomplishments, skills, values, and superpowers we've used throughout this chapter.

Accomplishments examples include:

- closed the books in fifteen days or less each month for the last twenty-four months, even during tax season;

- provided consistent and insightful ad hoc reporting to the leadership team;
- have run three half marathons a year for the last five years.

Skills examples include:

- deep knowledge in accounting best practices and principles;
- strong and consistent work ethic;
- data analytics expertise using multiple tools like Excel and Tableau.

Values examples include:

- My accounting team provides consistent and accurate accounting functions that are the core of business operations.
- I also provide accounting insights that help the leadership team make well-informed decisions.

Career superpowers examples include:

- strong knowledge of accounting systems and best practices used to consistently deliver high-quality core accounting functions
- provide deeper insights into the organization's status using analytics tools to deliver reporting whenever needed.

At first glance, it might feel like the domain experience in the example is a repeat of the earlier work related to skills, values, and accomplishments. It's not. Domain experience is an important lens through which you can look at your career, especially if you are seeking to make a significant switch in your career.

Thus far, you have detailed a lot of your work to help hiring managers and the job marketplace understand you. As you can see in the example above, an accounting professional with this background can easily make a case for another role in accounting. But what if they want to switch to a role in business analysis?

That's where domain experience is important. Domain experience highlights experiences that can apply universally to different roles: in this example, the domain experiences in accounting systems, analytics tools, and management reporting that correlates directly to a business analyst role. Further, they could be helpful for a role in a consulting firm.

Listing your domain experience is important so you can keep a higher-level view of your career, allowing you to consider more options and career directions.

Exercise: List Your Domain Experience

Write down in bullets or short sentences the experiences that apply to the roles, industries, and companies you want to pursue. Be as clear and concise as you can.

Crafting Your Brand Statement

By now you've inventoried your career through the different lenses and are ready to synopsize the results and insights you've gained. Remember, you are not bragging! So often we hear people express discomfort about this. A brand statement is meant to trigger further dialogue and conversation. It is not bragging, embellishing, or overstating. It's a statement of pride in accuracy in your career.

Sample Brand Statement

Let's use the examples we used in the domain experience section and view them together. As you look at them in total, what trends and patterns do you see? Those trends and patterns are the core of your brand statement. Here's an example of one that works:

Accomplishments

- Closed the books in fifteen days or less each month for the last twenty-four months, even during tax season;
- Provided consistent and insightful ad hoc reporting to the leadership team;
- Have run three half marathons a year for the last five years.

Skills

- Deep knowledge in accounting best practices and principles;
- Strong and consistent work ethic;
- Data analytics expertise using multiple tools like Excel and Tableau.

Values

- My accounting team provides consistent and accurate accounting functions that are the core of business operations.
- I also provide accounting insights that help the leadership team make well-informed decisions.

Career Superpowers

- Strong knowledge of accounting systems and best practices used to consistently deliver high-quality core accounting functions

- Provide deeper insights into the organization's status using analytics tools to deliver reporting whenever needed.

Domain Experience

- accounting systems
- analytics tools
- management reporting

Brand Statement

> I consistently deliver high-quality accounting services that are the core of my organization's operations. This also includes analysis and reporting that gives my leadership team stronger insights. I'm a "grinder" who believes my work and my passion for half marathon running are built around developing and honing my skills.

For this sample brand statement, we focused on consistency, strong accounting knowledge, and reporting. As a personal touch, we made a connection between the candidate's interest in running and their work. The "grinder" statement is a little colorful, but it continues to emphasize that this is someone who will get things done day in and day out.

Below are some real-world brand statement examples from our clients and program participants

"I implement big ideas. I am passionate about the transformations needed to make them happen and shepherding them to success. I have done this in materials R&D and now have moved into health care / public health."

"I am a problem-solver. I quickly dive deep into an organization, dissect the business problems, identify potential solutions, and work with key stakeholders to deliver desired results."

"An Internet of Things (IOT) native with expertise ranging from designing, building, and selling robotic industrial solutions as a start-up founding team member, to corporate development and strategic partnerships."

"Seasoned finance executive with more than a decade of investment experience in private equity, M&A, and corporate strategy. I direct and execute capital investments focused on primary and specialty medical group practices in support of my firm's growth strategies."

As you write your brand statement, here are a few additional guidelines to consider:

- Tie your statement to the most important pieces from your accomplishments, skills, values, and, most of all, your career superpowers.
- Blend them together into a cohesive message.
- Don't write more than 150 words. Get your message out, but don't go too deep.
- Don't obsess. Focus on just getting it down; you can worry about editing it later.
- Remember that your brand statement is not a résumé summary.

EXERCISE: WRITE YOUR BRAND STATEMENT'S FIRST DRAFT

Take all the work you've done and write out your first brand statement. It won't be perfect and might be wordy; that's fine. The important thing is to get your draft written out.

Getting Feedback

Now that you've finished your brand statement's first draft, we recommend you seek out feedback from a couple of sources. You're going to need different viewpoints, which will help you see yourself in different settings. You want your brand statement looked at from different angles to get a more holistic view. Choose a source for feedback who is:

- someone who knows you well—a friend, for example;
- a coworker, either past or present, or a professional acquaintance.

After you've finished gathering feedback on your brand statement, use the box below to summarize what you've learned. Even better, have your feedback partners write in it themselves.

As you're processing the feedback, here are some questions to consider:

- How did your feedback provider(s) describe you?
- What do you think you should add to your brand statement?
- What should you delete?

Exercise: Write Down Brand Statement Feedback

Write out ideas and comments that you want to incorporate into your brand statement.

Exercise: Write the Second Draft

Here are some guidelines for the final exercise:

- Add in feedback you found helpful.
- Make sure the feedback you added blends with the rest of your statement. Your writing should be cohesive.
- Ideally, your statement should be between 100 and 150 words.
- The key question for when you read it back should be: Does your brand statement feel comfortable to you?

Now collate the feedback you received and integrate it into the second draft of your brand statement.

The Job Search Manifesto process was a structured and pragmatic way to analyze and distill my prior accomplishments to develop my brand so I could effectively communicate who I was, what I was able to bring, and what I was looking for in my discussions at Google. Getting people to understand my career goals and relevant skills in informational interviews prior to applying was particularly helpful, as the feedback and recommendations I received (people to follow up with, teams I may find interesting, business problems needing solved) were tailor fit and significantly accelerated my search to find a role suited to me in such a large company.

Eric Roe

Summary

Describing yourself to the outside world should be less intimidating once you work through the exercises in this chapter.

- Your brand statement is a core piece of your job search and career development. It's your answer to the question, "Tell me about yourself."
- You will also use it in your LinkedIn profile, résumé, and in communication when you reach out to build and deepen business relationships.
- You start by building a detailed inventory of your superpowers, domain experience, and most relevant achievements as they relate to your target.
- That information will let you craft an effective and memorable brand statement. It's a pitch that opens with a unique hook, illustrates your relevant skills and experience, highlights an apt achievement, and stimulates further conversations and connections.
- Your brand statement is always evolving. Don't be afraid to update it and repeat these exercises at least once a year.

RELATIONSHIP BUILDING AND NETWORKING

Manifesto

- Building relationships instead of networking is a key part of the job search and your career.
- Networking is not transactional nor all about you.
- Relationship building is long term, mutually beneficial , and built on trust.

Raul's Reach-Out Plan Deepened His Career Options

During the two decades Raul spent at a Fortune 10 company, he held customer-facing roles in sales and channel management, along with being a sales training leader. When layoffs were announced, Raul knew his job was at risk. It wasn't long before he was told that he was being let go in ninety days.

He was frustrated and stressed, but he decided to use career coaching to help build a job search action plan. Raul had a strong foundation to build on: his business relationships. His work over two decades at the company was based around a specific business area. Raul knew the customers and resellers well. Additionally, he knew a lot of good people who had left the company and joined other great organizations. The core of his job search was reaching out to this community.

Raul spent time building his brand statement, revising his LinkedIn profile, and, finally, updating his résumé. But he started reaching out even before that was all done. Making contact and getting in dialogue was critical to him. In fact, he started reaching out once he had a comfortable brand statement. He revised his LinkedIn profile several times, integrating what he learned from his reach-outs.

He also used career coaching to update his résumé, first building a base résumé that we would adjust to match specific roles. He didn't begin work on his résumé immediately, instead focusing more time on building relationships. Later he created role-specific résumés modified from his base résumé.

His reach-out strategy was simple: he let people know he was being laid off in a few months and that he wanted to get their thoughts and ideas on directions he might consider. Raul didn't ask for lots of action steps, just thoughts and ideas. These conversations began while he was still working and continued for several months after his layoff. The results were solid and encouraging.

People wanted to help and offered much more than just ideas. Raul was introduced to key leaders (including the CEO of a well-known tech company) and was referred to more than half a dozen roles in multiple companies.

Raul never blindly applied for a job. He had an internal sponsor or advocate lined up each time. Job boards were helpful for information gathering, but he spent most of his time in conversation.

Shortly he found himself in multiple interviews; at one time he was deep in the interview process for four roles simultaneously. He had moments of doubt and was turned down multiple times.

Ultimately, he landed in a role just a few months after his layoff. The company liked Raul's skills and experience so much they offered him two roles to consider. He chose one and has been growing his career there, but he's also keeping in touch with his most important career asset: his business relationships.

About This Chapter

It's easy to read Raul's story and think he's fortunate to have a deep and ready-to-access community. But that view discounts the two decades he spent at one company building relationships one at a time and keeping those relationships alive. Building and nurturing business relationships is essential to a job search and career success. This was not a natural approach for Raul, who was not outgoing, but he made keeping in touch with his business relationships an ongoing part of his life.

People are often told that résumé building and reactive job submissions (e.g., online applications) should be the main area they should focus on when they're looking for work. We disagree. Business relationships are the most important part of a job search.

David Burkus, author of *Friend of a Friend . . . Understanding the Hidden Networks That Transform Your Life and Your Career*, said it best: "Knowing who your friends are and who their friends are, so you can gain a better understanding of the community, will lead to better odds that your network will enhance your success." (10)

Here's a safe, incremental plan, built on practice and success. The focus: start with familiar, local people and move outward to

- friends and coworkers
- acquaintances and referrals (weak ties) and
- leaders and admired people.

Friends and coworkers already know you and are naturally inclined to assist. They're also great people to share your story with. Encourage them to comment on your thoughts and ideas. This makes it easier to move on to people with whom you have less of a direct relationship.

Moving to the next group, these are classic weak ties; people you knew at some point but have not been in close contact with are examples. Finally, move on to leaders or even people you admire. Getting comfortable with reaching out, and with having these dialogues, is the core of a job search and your career success.

You'll notice that we've been avoiding using the term "networking." This word comes with a lot of baggage and preconceived ideas (such as being strictly transactional), so we prefer to call this step relationship building.

Because job changing has increased over the past few decades, growing and maintaining connections is more important than ever. Additionally, relationship building goes beyond your job search. Keeping your networks active enhances your personal life as well as your career.

This will be one of the longer sections in *The Job Search Manifesto*. In it we'll cover the types of contacts you have, as listed above, and will identify high-impact contacts in each relationship group, including:

- developing the content necessary to reach out;
- designing a plan to reach out; and
- executing your plan through connecting and sharing.

Friend of a Friend is a terrific book that streamlines the process of deciding whom to contact, focusing on weak ties. As noted above, these are the people whom you know but have lost touch with. Often, they have a different view of the marketplace and how your skills and experiences might fit more broadly than you had considered.

Acquaintances and referrals are the core of weak ties. Having practiced with friends and coworkers, it is easier to reach out and engage with these less familiar people. This is the major group you should focus your communication on.

Types of Contacts: Active and Dormant, Strong and Weak

Throughout our lives, we may form thousands of relationships, although research suggests we typically only have one to two active relationships at any time. During a job search, our inclination is to reach out primarily to these active relationships. These are divided into two groups: strong ties and weak ties. A third category, consisting of people you've lost contact with, is known as your dormant ties.

Strong Ties

Strong ties are deep relationships made up of the "go-to people" who have your back. These relationships have a strong trust base. Both parties are motivated to help each other. In a job search, this is where we typically start.

As you consider your strong ties, keep in mind that they may have a blind spot about you. They may only know you from one aspect of your life and may also be strong advocates for you. What's wrong with that?

That support is great, but they may not have unique insight into your career. Also, they may have a positive bias about you that can cloud their opinions and ideas. They may not be able to help you in a career transition. Examples of strong ties include:

- coworker or team member
- neighbor
- sports team member or other hobby activity partner
- friend
- family member

Weak Ties

The key difference in a weak-tie relationship is its depth. These are people with whom you have a polite, friendly, but non-deep relationship. At first glance, they may not seem important, but there's a lot of value to your weak ties. Weak ties can help you build bridges to different groups. They also can provide new insights, fresh thinking, and unique information.

Weak ties may not know you well, but their unique view can be critically helpful in a job search. They can be a bridge into new groups and networks. Examples of weak ties include:

- coworker from another team or business unit
- former coworker
- classmate

- customer or vendor
- someone with a shared sports or arts interest, but not on the same team or group
- distant family member

Dormant Ties

Dormant ties can be strong or weak ties that you have simply lost contact with. These are good people that you knew, but life got in the way of continued contact. Research shows that dormant ties—especially dormant strong ties—can be easily reactivated. Often, these are the people you reconnect with right away and feel like it's only been a few days since you last spoke. And remember, dormant weak ties also have value, if approached correctly.

Now that you have the basics of who to reach out to, here's a strategy and approach to reaching out.

Reach-Out Strategy—Three Conversation Tracks

In job search and career development, we've recognized that it's not only important who you reach out to but also how you reach out. This mix of who you reach out to, why you reach out to them, and how to do this effectively has been a frequent challenge for many people we've coached. We have condensed these ideas down to three reach-out methods or tracks.

Touch track: stay in contact or relationship support. This is the core of a successful career: staying in touch and supporting existing relationships. These are usually existing strong ties or weak ties that you want to become strong ties.

Explore track: career learning and relationship building. These are usually weak ties or dormant ties, but they can also be strong ties. The track's objective is to build relationships based on the topic of careers and current business conditions.

Role-specific track: relationship development focused on a specific career or job request. This is similar to the explore track, but it is more targeted around a specific role or organization. Often, you're requesting that the person sponsor or refer you for a specific role.

We'll detail the steps for the touch and explore tracks in this chapter; the role-specific track will be covered in the chapter on job search execution.

Conversation Tracks

Here's a quick summary of the conversation tracks we've just discussed.

TRACK	DESCRIPTION AND TOPIC	STRONG TIES	WEAK TIES
Touch	Staying connected, general updates, practice		

Explore	State of the job market, company information, role information		
Role-specific	State of the job market, company information, specific job information		

You're going to use your memory—and, most importantly, LinkedIn—for this exercise. From now on, LinkedIn will be the key tool for your job search. As you'll find in the rest of the book, LinkedIn allows you to complete three important functions:

- identify and reach out to strong and weak ties, both active and dormant
- build a compelling LinkedIn profile that will attract recruiters and hiring managers
- search for and apply to jobs.

EXERCISE: IDENTIFY KEY RELATIONSHIPS

- Write down as many relationships as you can and indicate the following:
    - which part of your life they come from?
    - what kind of tie they are (also note if they are dormant)?

NAME	Personal	Professional	Tie	Dormant

It's always daunting to consider reaching out to a large list, so we'll pare it down and focus on just five. The next exercise will make your first reach-out simple and comfortable.

EXERCISE: FIRST REACH-OUT

From the list above, identify five strong ties and then have an informal conversation. The goal is to just get comfortable with discussing your job search with people who care about and respect you.

During the conversation, try sharing your brand statement. It's a chance to practice speaking about it. Check in on how they are doing. Keep the conversation fifty-fifty between you and them; don't monopolize the dialogue.

Your first outreach should be easy and comfortable. This is a chance to do a warm-up for your job search.

Use the form below to keep a list of the strong ties you've spoken with and how the conversation went. Capture your thoughts in the Discussion column.

NAME	Track	Tie	Discussion
	Touch	Strong	
	Touch	Strong	
	Touch	Strong	
	Touch	Strong	
	Touch	Strong	
	Touch	Strong	
	Touch	Strong	
	Touch	Strong	
	Touch	Strong	
	Touch	Strong	

After you've had some or all of these first conversations, let's look at what you've learned. Here are some questions to help process and synthesize. Let's make it more formal by building a reach-out message.

You'll be crafting a simple, easy-to-read email that makes a good case that someone should speak with you. Remember, this isn't a sales pitch, just a chance to speak with someone you respect and value.

To make this process easier, build the following exercises around a real person. Select one person from your weak-tie list. You should come away from the exercise with a ready to use reach-out template.

Create Your Reach-Out Message

There are three components in a reach-out email message. We'll describe them below and will then walk you through a series of exercises to build the idea out. Your reach-out email will consist of the hook, your brand, and your "ask."

Like many components of the job search manifesto, this is an iterative process. As you learn more from your responses, adjust each of the elements of your reach-out email.

The Hook—Your Reason for Reaching Out

Your hook is what you have in common (shared background, people, and/or experiences) with the person you're reaching out to. If it's a common interest area, be specific on what that area is.

One way to demonstrate that common area is by referring to something they've done, including a talk, presentation, article, or post—something that shows you know their background and you've done your homework.

If it's a common acquaintance or friend, make sure to explain what you've learned about them from the friend or acquaintance.

In all cases, be upbeat but don't exaggerate or oversell.

This should not be long, about fifty to seventy-five words. Aim to do this in two sentences, three sentences max. Here's an example:

> I'm a second-year exec MBA student at Wharton San Francisco, focused on marketing. I attended your recent talk at the Wharton entrepreneurship workshop on "Building a Start-Up" and came away impressed with your team's success. Your expertise in start-ups led me to reach out.

EXERCISE: WRITE YOUR HOOK

Use the guidelines discussed above and write out your hook. Aim for fifty to seventy-five words in two sentences, three sentences max. Brevity is important.

Brand Statement—Identify Yourself

This will be the second paragraph of your email. Here we'll use your brand statement work again. You want to keep this short and, ideally, focused on where you and the contact share common traits.

This should be three to four sentences max. If necessary, adjust your brand statement to emphasize where your brand has commonality with the other person. Here's an example:

> I'm currently a director of product management at Company X. I've led teams in product development, operations, and market execution for some of Company X's most successful products, including Product A and Product B.

EXERCISE: WRITE YOUR BRAND STATEMENT

Write a brief form of your brand statement here. Find commonality you share with the receiver.

Your Ask

The core of the request is your ask. We often see clients get tongue-tied on the ask, but it is really straightforward. The key parts of the ask are:

- stating a specific reason for the conversation
- making sure the request is relevant to the other person
- making it simple for the other party: you'll do all the set-up work
- being realistic, sincere, and flexible in the tone of the note and your actions
- thanking them for their consideration

It's important that *you* handle the logistics, not them. Keep the dialogue short, for example, a ten-to fifteen-minute call. Show respect for them and their time. Here's an example:

> I'd greatly appreciate a chance to briefly talk about growth marketing, especially in consumer products. Your direct experience and your thoughts about trends and challenges would be extremely helpful. I can share current thoughts and research as well.
>
> A phone call would be great, or coffee—whatever is best for you and your time. Please let me know if you can connect in the next two weeks, and I'll work around your schedule.

EXERCISE: WRITE YOUR ASK

Share what you have in common, in fifty to seventy-five words and two to three sentences.

Don't hesitate to ask follow-up questions on thoughts and ideas they share. Ask clarifying questions that will help you integrate. Use the information to explain again your core reason for connecting.

Write a Compelling Email or InMail Subject Line

Email marketing is big business, so we looked at research in that field. AWeber, a top email marketing company, has analyzed one thousand emails from one hundred top marketers to determine how experts send emails. They found that over 80 percent send emails with subject lines of sixty characters or less. This is important, since many email applications don't show full subject lines longer than that. Subject lines averaged 43.85 characters long. (11)

Career Contessa has four solid subject-line recommendations, based on the situation:

- There's a common connection: "Susan, Denice Lewis recommended I reach out"
- They have public content (talks, blog posts, podcasts, or articles): "Samuel, I loved your LinkedIn article on customer lifecycles"
- Value is offered: "Product manager with B2B expertise interested in helping your team"
- A question is posed: "Any advice for someone who loves the marketing work you're doing at Company X?" (12)

Best Practices on Timing

You won't get 100 percent responses, but let's do everything you can to keep your response rate high. Here are three recommendations from LinkedIn, which is based on their inbox response research:

- The best time is between nine and ten in the morning local time for the recipient; you are 12 percent more likely to get a response if you send your email at this time.
- The best day is Thursday.
- Don't send InMails (LinkedIn's proprietary email system) over the weekend! InMail messages sent on Saturdays are 16 percent less likely to get a response compared to those sent earlier in the work week. (11)

One caveat is emailing recruiters. Our busiest day as recruiters is Monday. That's when we review and process new applications from the weekend, schedule our screening calls for the week, and keep on pace with the previous week's activities. Reach out to recruiters all day Tuesday through Friday noon, their time.

Meeting and Follow-Up Plan Statement

When you meet or speak on the phone, remember that it's a conversation, not a pitch. Focus on listening; you're meeting to hear their thoughts and ideas. Be prepared and have questions ready. Here are some examples:

- What drew you to your role/company/industry?
- What were some key career decisions you've made?
- What makes you optimistic about this role/company/industry?
- What concerns do you have about this role/company/industry?

- What ideas or advice do you have for someone interested in this role/company/industry?

Treat this as a conversation and ask follow-up questions, especially on the topics you find interesting.

Even if this is a casual conversation, the other party may also be evaluating your fit for a role in their organization, or might have other ideas. There's no need to make a heavy-handed request to be sponsored or to have them submit you directly. Here are two ways to wrap up the conversation:

- "I really appreciate what you've shared; it's been very helpful. What next steps do you recommend?"
- "From what you've shared, it seems like my next steps should be to do X, Y, and Z. What do you think?"

Following Up

With the tone you set by asking open questions about the industry, role, or company; their journey; and a brief set of action steps, following up should be straightforward and easy.

Your immediate follow-up is to send a thank-you within one or two days after you've spoken. It doesn't have to be long, just a few sentences that follow this structure:

- Start with a sincere thank-you.
- Mention one or two takeaways from the conversation.
- State your next action steps.
- Close with another thank-you.

There's a second follow-up opportunity that people often forget: letting the person know your progress. This is particularly important if they have referred you into a role either in their organization or another. Letting them know about your progress is a sign of appreciation and respect.

"I wouldn't have gotten my current job without building extensive relationships and keeping them warm over the years, and I've made mistakes in the past not seeking additional data points from contacts and just made career decisions based on my own."

Shyvee Shi

Building a Reach-Out Plan

Now that you've done some initial outreach, let's put this into production. Building a reach-out plan should be an ongoing part of a job search. Frankly, it should be an ongoing part of a successful career.

With that in mind, the following table is a planning document. Earlier in the chapter you selected five people whom you knew well and could experiment with. Now we want you to broaden your approach, looking at multiple activity paths and both strong and weak ties.

Use the exercise below to identify ten people you will reach out to in the next week. Ideally this will become a weekly habit. Over time you should be reaching out to more weak ties than strong ties.

We can't emphasize enough that a continuous and sustainable reach-out plan has to be the core of your job search. It's also a skill set, and you will get better as you continue.

People often experience hesitation, particularly if they're introverted or not outgoing. We want you to execute, but don't feel you have to be really outgoing to do this. Many of our clients are shy, but this is a safe way to develop outreach skills.

As a reminder, here are the conversation tracks and how they often connect to strong and weak ties.

TRACK	DESCRIPTION AND TOPIC	STRONG TIES	WEAK TIES
Touch	Staying connected, general updates, practice		
Explore	State of the job market, company information, role information		
Role-specific	State of the job market, company information, specific job information		

EXERCISE: BUILD A ONE-WEEK REACH-OUT LIST

List contacts you want to reach out to, including the track and what kind of tie they are. After you speak with them, make a note of the discussion.

NAME	TRACK	TIE	DISCUSSION

Be optimistic but realistic. We've seen clients and people in our programs get about 30 percent response rates. MailChimp did a detailed study on the percentage of emails that were opened. Across all industries, they found overall that 22.71 percent of emails were opened. (13)

Target Three to Five Conversations per Week

It takes a week or two to get responses and start scheduling conversations, but we like our clients to have three to five conversations per week, depending on their overall activity. This will take a few weeks to develop. The first week's reach-out exercise has ten reach-outs, assuming not everyone will get back to you right away.

If you are still in a job and have a busy schedule, three conversations is a good sustainable goal. We'll discuss this more in later chapters.

The key theme in building relationships is to take it in steps and build on each win. Building these relationships shouldn't end when you get your next job; this needs to be an ongoing process.

These relationships will help in both the short and long term. Plus, you stay connected to others, which is especially helpful in the tense, isolated world of the COVID-19 pandemic.

Summary

- Effectively reaching out to your existing relationships and building new relationships are core activities for your job search. In this chapter we've outlined that process in a way that will make it easy to achieve, even if you're a bit shy and introverted.

- You built and organized a contact strategy consisting of strong ties that open doors to weak ties and dormant ties. All these contacts will expand your network and lead to job opportunities.

- Adjusting your brand statement according to your specific outreach target lets you create unique conversation tracks and strategies for each unique interaction.

- The three conversation tracks—touch, explore, and role-specific—each have specific agendas that will help you organize informative and comfortable conversations.

- We've provided a model on how to structure a reach-out note. The three parts are hook, brand, and the ask. With these, sending effective notes becomes easier, and they will be better received.

- An often forgotten but equally important aspect of the reach-out is to create a comprehensive and personal follow-up strategy.

SOURCING

JOB SEARCH PLANNING

Manifesto

- Think of a job search as a marketing project that develops both warm and cold leads.
- Just sending in a résumé for a job post is like cold-calling—the success rate is low.
- Most recruiters are focused on filling positions immediately. Understand that these positions are often just transactional.

Samuel: Career Change and a Blog

Samuel worked in consumer banking branches for most of his career. Now in his late thirties, he wanted to step away and join the tech sector. He'd become fascinated with the melding of technology and finance, a fast-growing technology segment known as Fintech. Samuel intensely read up on Fintech and took it a step further—he started a Fintech blog.

The blog was mostly a collection of Fintech articles and his analyses of their content. It was more of a passion project, but it spurred him to use career coaching to help him make a transition to aFfintech company.

Samuel worked through all *The Job Search Manifesto* steps but also strategized how to use his blog as a unique tool in his job search. Since he was already researching the Fintech industry and writing blog posts, Samuel added an extra step to track each company's open positions and note their senior leadership. He also leveraged his blog to reach out to frontline leaders and build solid business relationships with them.

When applying for a role, Samuel reached out to a senior leader. He not only described his fit for the job but also included a link to his blog. The method paid off.

Samuel found a FinTech start-up that had posted a role in operations, and he applied. He didn't just send in a résumé but reached out to the CEO by explaining his background, showing interest in the job, and sending a link to his blog. A recruiter reached out, and after a phone screen, Samuel was invited on-site for a group interview.

The format was a panel interview that included the CEO, the recruiter, and an operations manager. The interview team quickly picked up that Samuel had a strong understanding of the FinTech world. His communication skills also stood out. The CEO was distracted throughout the interview, often looking at his laptop versus directly engaging in the conversation. But overall, Samuel felt he did well.

The recruiter contacted him shortly after the interview and told him the CEO had apologized for being distracted but was dealing with a lot of sales-lead issues. Given Samuel's industry knowledge and communication skills, the CEO wanted to offer Samuel a job, but not in operations. The team felt Samuel would be a strong salesperson, but he would have to start in an entry-level role.

Samuel analyzed the role and the compensation, evaluating both by using his career values, and decided the role was too good to pass up. The offer was lower than his current income, but the hit was not severe and there were lots of upsides both financially and experientially. The decision paid off. Samuel not only closed sales but also helped organize the onboarding process for future sales team members.

It also helped that he had built several solid business relationships from his blog. He used those contacts to help build his sales pipeline. Samuel continues to write his blog and share it on LinkedIn and other sites.

About This Chapter

In Samuel's job search, simply sending a résumé was not going to work. He was making a big career transition and had to make a strong case before he even applied. His online presence had to show strong knowledge in the Fintech industry. That's why the blog was so helpful.

With a career transition that included both a role and industry change, coaching helped Samuel understand how to effectively use all the sources that help identify and support a job search.

We've broken up the job search process into two chapters: planning (this chapter) and execution. Each part is equally important, and they are deeply linked to the other chapters in the book.

This chapter provides a baseline for setting up your search, including how to connect and interface with recruiters. We also want you to adjust your view of a job search as a one-dimensional process.

The search for jobs becomes easier if you view it as a marketing project. In marketing, you have two types of leads: warm leads and cold leads. Another analogy is the magnet versus the megaphone.

Cold leads are much like a cold call, where you reach out to a person or a company and hope they might reach back out to you. You are either blindly submitting your résumé to job posts, waiting for a recruiter to reach out, or both. In each approach, you have no control. You are waiting for someone else to act. Unfortunately, this is the job search norm.

Warm leads are potential customers who've expressed interest in the product or service.

This chapter will focus more on planning and understanding the most effective steps you can take in your job search. We'll be poking holes in some of the more common job search steps that are largely ineffective.

Be a Magnet not a Megaphone

According to blogger Kayla Matthews:

> Outbound marketing . . . seeks to reach as many people as possible with one blanket message. Inbound marketing is the attempt to reach out to the individual with a carefully tailored message and, if possible, to inspire that individual to respond by reaching out to you. If outbound marketing is a megaphone, inbound marketing is a magnet. (11)

Some effective inbound or magnet marketing methods include (also according to Matthews) "sharing insightful content, becoming a thought leader in their field, and targeting specific prospects by educating themselves on what those clients are looking for"; the Magnet approach "draws people closer by building a relationship of trust and knowledge." (11)

Don't be like this:

- Submitting résumés blindly to online job posts; also known as "Press, send, and pray"
- Waiting for or working exclusively with recruiters

Submitting Résumés Blindly

Applying for a job has become incredibly simple, but it's a classic megaphone job search step. Blind résumé submissions have become incredibly easy. Applicant tracking systems (ATSs), the foundational tool used in recruiting/talent acquisition, are designed to make submissions very simple and fast: minimal data entry with point-and-click speed.

With this ease of use, anyone can apply for any position—and that's a core problem. Recruiting organizations are now inundated with inappropriate candidates. As much as you hear about bots and artificial intelligence (AI), recruiting staffs must still look at and make some determination on each of these résumés. You are one of hundreds if not thousands who have applied for these roles.

Mike and his internal recruiting team often dreaded Monday mornings. Résumés that had been submitted from Friday to Sunday evening took most of Monday morning—if not the entire day—to process. And for popular positions, the submission volume generally stays high for several weeks after posting. So, here's the question: Do you want yours to be one of those résumés that has to be processed and treated like everyone else's?

Working with Recruiters

Both of us were recruiters, so you won't hear us slam the industry. But we want to educate you on the best practices if you work with them. To do that, let's break down the industry and how it works. First, there are two types of recruiters: external and internal.

External recruiters are individuals or recruiting agencies who work on behalf of the company to fill one or more positions. What's important about external recruiters is their business model, which is based on how they get paid. The business models are *contingent*, *retained*, and *executive*.

Contingent Recruiters - These recruiters are compensated like real estate agents, paid only when the deal is closed. If you're working with a contingent recruiter, you are the deal.

Contingent recruiters focus on speed to hire, a large candidate pool, and always searching for the next position to fill. Due to the nature of how they're paid, contingent recruiting is a transactional numbers game. As a candidate this means you will only get feedback and activity if you are qualified for a current position they are trying to fill. The only feedback you'll get is how to improve your résumé and some pointers on interviewing. Also, contingent recruiters may not have in-depth information about the role, company, or leadership team.

The percentages are dropping, but contingent recruiters typically receive 20 percent of the candidate's annual salary.

They do not receive compensation for equity, RSUs (restricted stock units), or sign-on bonuses.

Retained Recruiters - These are usually more experienced recruiters, often working more senior positions and receiving an initial payment up front with a percentage bonus when a candidate accepts an offer. This means that retained recruiters have a more stable cash flow and can spend a bit more time on their search. For the candidate this means a little more feedback and more in-depth information about the role in the company.

Executive recruiters are also retained, but they are focused on senior leadership positions. Their initial payment is higher, and often their percentage on the back end is higher. Executive recruiters will sometimes receive options. They are the most detailed of all recruiters in their screening and candidate preparation. Usually they are focused on VP to C-level roles.

These recruiters have done good assessments of the organizations and will provide a lot of information. They are also strong in candidate preparation. Finally, executive recruiters are often the most experienced recruiters, and some can give you good information about industries.

Internal or Corporate Recruiters - These are employees of the company they recruit for, and there are several advantages to working with them. First, they can understand both the role and the company better than an external recruiter can. Second, they can explain and are involved directly in the hiring process. Third, they are better able to position you and prep you for phone screens and face-to-face interviews.

There are three main functions of an internal recruiting team: *sourcing*, *recruiting*, and *coordination*. In working with a larger company and their recruiting team, you may be interacting with multiple recruiters, each supporting one or more of these activities.

But many corporate recruiters have more than a full plate. We know corporate recruiters who are simultaneously working more than two dozen job requisitions at once. They are very busy, and it can show when you're waiting for feedback or next steps. Though this is not an excuse, that is often a corporate recruiter's world.

Recruiter Limitations and Best Practices

Whether external or internal, remember that recruiters are *not* career coaches. A candidate receiving detailed plans, comments on résumés, practices for interviewing, and in-depth feedback from a recruiter is rare. If you are not hired, then feedback will be almost nonexistent, mainly for legal reasons.

Here's the essential information and action steps to manage working with recruiters, either external or internal:

- Get crystal clear on the hiring process.
- Understand the organization's time lines and urgency.
- Ask about the candidate pool.

We'll go into detail on these steps below. Also be sure to trust but verify and to control submissions with external recruiters.

Get Crystal Clear on the Hiring Process

Ask questions to clearly understand the hiring process. You want to know the steps they will follow and who is involved at each step.

Example: You will do a phone screen with the recruiter. If you pass, you'll have a phone screen with the hiring manager. If the hiring manager feels that you likely fit the role, they will bring you on-site to meet, along with three or four team members and another leader in the organization. The process will take about four hours. Each person will meet you separately. A recruiting coordinator will manage scheduling.

The questions you should ask are:

- What are the steps in your hiring process?
- Who is involved in each step?
- For an on-site interview, how many people are involved?
- Who are the interviewers? (Ask this so you can research them before you meet.)
- Who coordinates the process, how long will it take, and when will they reach out to schedule?

Understand the Organization's Time Lines and Urgency

Countless times we've seen candidates get really frustrated by a long hiring process. Much of that frustration could have been eliminated by asking up front about the organization's time line and their urgency to fill the role.

The best person to ask is the recruiter, and a simple way to do that is to ask, "What day does the company want this person to start?" Notice that this is specific, which is the goal; the more specific, the better.

Don't be stunned if the answer comes back "as soon as possible." The organization is likely still figuring that out. The answer that could raise an eyebrow would be, "We are in the early stages of the hiring process." This tells you the process will take a while.

Ask about the Candidate Pool

This is a question that some people find uncomfortable, but as recruiters we had no problem being asked. In fact, it's helpful that both sides are clear. When you ask, "How many candidates are in your candidate pool?" you'll have clarity on how long the hiring process may take. Of course, you'll also learn how the competitive the role is. As recruiters, we aimed for a candidate pool of three to five, depending on the complexity of the role.

Here's the better way…be a magnet

- Maintaining strong ties or your existing network
- Weak ties—expanding your network
- Dormant ties—reaching out and reactivating relationships

The Better Way to Apply to a Job Posting

Yes, we want you to apply to job postings, but we don't want it to be the only activity in your job search. There should be an emphasis on "megaphone" activities with applying for jobs as part of your job search activity mix. But we advocate you take a blended approach that includes applying with targeted outreach.

Applying to a job posting should not be just sending in your résumé and waiting. A leader at a major tech company made this statement to us: "Just applying for a job on our site is like throwing your résumé into the abyss."

In other words: you need to do more.

Adjust your résumé to align with the role. The first three to four requirements for the role are typically the most important. Clearly indicate in your résumé which bullet points you have done. Use their terminology in your résumé to describe your matching experience and skills.

Adjust your LinkedIn profile, *if needed.* We'll cover your LinkedIn profile in the next chapter, and you probably won't need to make many changes. The exception is if the role is significantly different from your recent roles. In that case, you will need to explain how your work aligns with the new role.

Find an internal advocate to sponsor you. Finding a sponsor is key and uses many of the same methods discussed in the chapter on relationship building. This may require a little detective work, and you ideally want a strong-tie connection to refer or sponsor you. If there isn't a strong tie, stretch a bit to reach out to a weak tie.

If you have no success there, reach out to a recruiter. The bottom line is that you should never apply to a job posting without reaching out to someone in the organization.

Job Posting Action Plan

Let's use the concepts in this chapter on a real job posting you are interested in. You'll make changes to your résumé, possibly add content to your LinkedIn profile, and then identify potential advocates in the organization.

In the chapter on job search execution, we cover in detail the hands-on pieces of the reach-out emails and more. The next exercise will help you organize your job search.

EXERCISE: BUILD A JOB POSTING PLAN

In the table below, write out the job post details. Then look at LinkedIn to see who your strong ties are.

Then find weak ties. Use the weak-tie ideas from the relationship-building chapter but also consider leaders or staff in the group to which the role belongs.

TARGET ROLE	**Organization:** **Date posted:**
Résumé updates:	
LinkedIn updates (if needed)	
Advocates: strong ties	
Advocates: weak ties	
Recruiters	

Summary

- We had a vital mission for this chapter: to break people out of applying for roles as their only job search action. The concept of the magnet versus the microphone was meant to explain having multiple activities that don't strictly rely on others.

- The ideas on how to work with recruiters are also important. Yes, they are gatekeepers, but understanding how to work with them and how they operate is also important.

- The final part of the chapter tied the concepts together for a real job post. The exercise of doing research about the job post should be the new way you apply for roles.

- This is the research and planning side of your job search. In a later chapter we will discuss job search execution in greater detail. But you should be leaving this chapter with a more well-rounded view of how to plan your job search. This will make your execution faster and stronger.

LINKEDIN

Manifesto

- Your LinkedIn profile is more important to your job search than your résumé.
- The "About" section of your LinkedIn profile is the most important section.
- You must answer the question, "Can I explain my successes and experience in a way other people understand?"

David: Layoff and LinkedIn

After working with an organization for more than a decade, David walked into the office, was escorted into a conference room, and was promptly laid off. Suddenly, he was back on the job market.

With an engineering degree, an MBA, and a long and successful career as a program manager behind him, David had a strong background. Working against him was a LinkedIn profile and résumé that were out of date and too generic.

To build his confidence and learn how to navigate the job search, David began career coaching. Through coaching, David worked on developing and executing his unique job search plan and focused on his LinkedIn profile.

Coaching began by crafting David's brand statement. As mentioned earlier in the book, the brand statement is the first paragraph of the About section. David's brand statement was the opening for his LinkedIn About section.

After creating David's brand statement, Mike asked David to deepen his LinkedIn About section in one of two ways. His key work on his LinkedIn profile included:

- describing key wins and experiences
- detailing his strengths and attributes;
- making sure the strengths and attributes mirrored what was in demand or needed in the roles for which he wanted to apply.

David chose to focus on his strengths and attributes, then crafted four short stories that highlighted his affinity for teamwork, his knack for solving problems, and his ability to bring complex products to market. The stories were brief: around two to three sentences each.

To help recruiters find him, David concluded his About section with a brief list of key terms in the form of a quick additional summary.

David's LinkedIn still needed work, but he put the edits up right away. It wasn't necessary to wait until everything was completed. With the revised profile, David was contacted by multiple recruiters, and his LinkedIn activity dramatically increased.

After several interviews (he was a finalist for two or three roles) with different companies, a large publicly traded company hired David as a program manager.

Now that he's employed, David's focus has shifted to career success, and he continues to keep his LinkedIn profile updated.

About This Chapter

According to LinkedIn, 90 percent of recruiters with LinkedIn accounts are on LinkedIn daily. And based on our experience, they often spend several hours a day reviewing profiles.

Based on our recruiting experience, we strongly believe that your LinkedIn profile is more important than your résumé. We know this because we have lived it.

As recruiters, we found 20 to 30 percent of our candidates on LinkedIn. Many of those hires started as passive candidates; they weren't actively looking for a new role, but they kept their LinkedIn profiles current.

Frequently, we didn't even ask the people we found on LinkedIn for their résumés. Their online profiles were enough. LinkedIn makes it remarkably simple for recruiters to capture LinkedIn profiles into their ATSs instead of using résumés.

In addition to recruiters, hiring managers and other leaders use LinkedIn to look for job candidates. Frequently these leaders would send profiles for our recruiting team to look over and reach out to.

Now let's talk about what recruiters see when they look at your profile and what you should emphasize.

How Recruiters See You

This is a public LinkedIn profile that comes up when you search for someone. This is *not* what a recruiter sees. Note: all screenshots in this chapter have been altered for privacy protection.

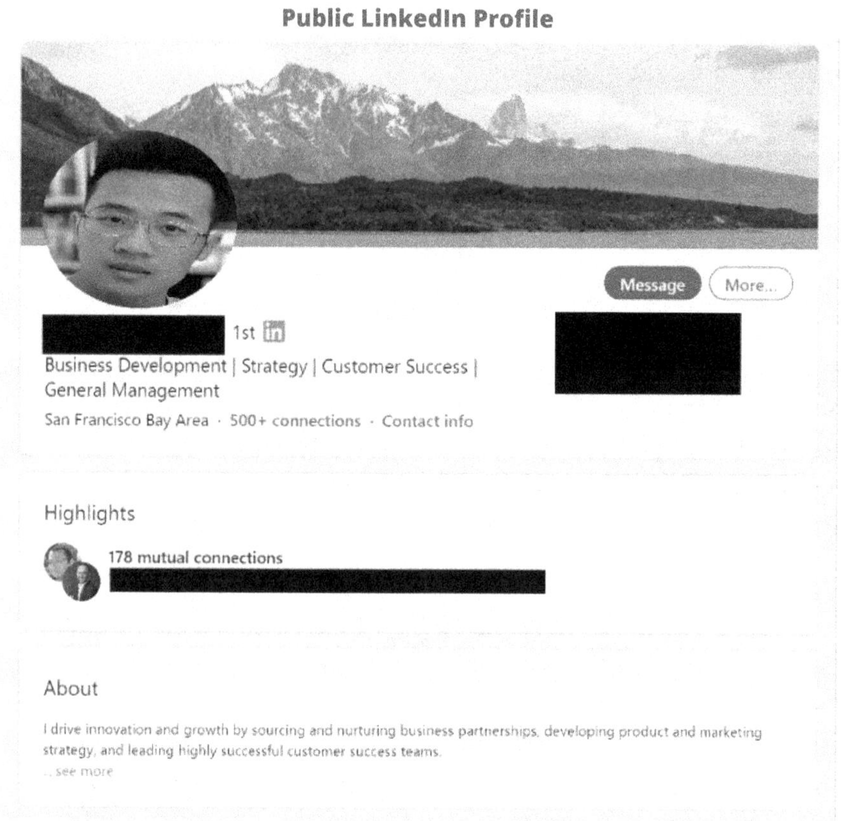

LinkedIn provides recruiters with tools to filter their searches. Recruiters also have a unique display when viewing profiles (which they can then download and add to their ATSs).

This is important: *LinkedIn Recruiter's tools make it so profiles look different to recruiters.* Recruiters, hiring managers, and other leaders are the major audience your profile reaches. The key to LinkedIn is knowing how they see your profile.

Here's a screenshot of the LinkedIn Recruiter search screen and search categories—it's extensive!

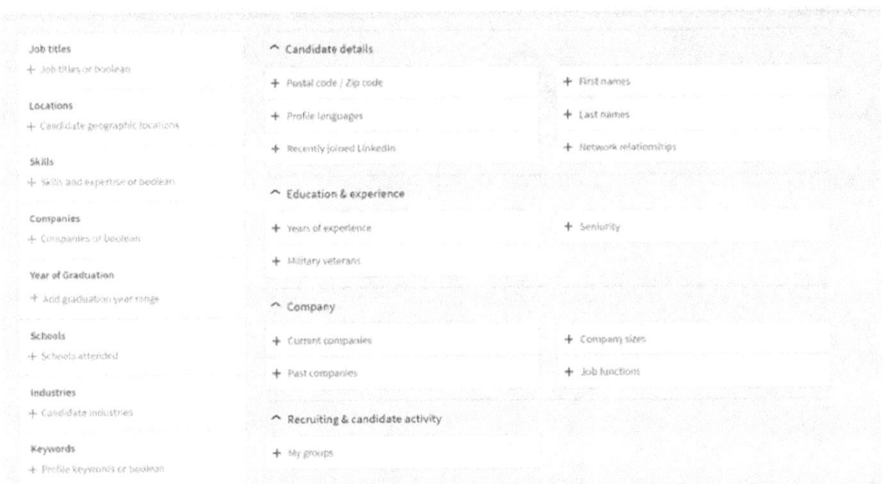

LinkedIn Recruiter Screen

As recruiters, we would usually start our search by adjusting the options in the left column. If the first search yielded a lot of candidates, we would narrow the results down by adjusting the options on the right.

The next page shows an example of the results screen from a search.

LinkedIn Recruiter results screen

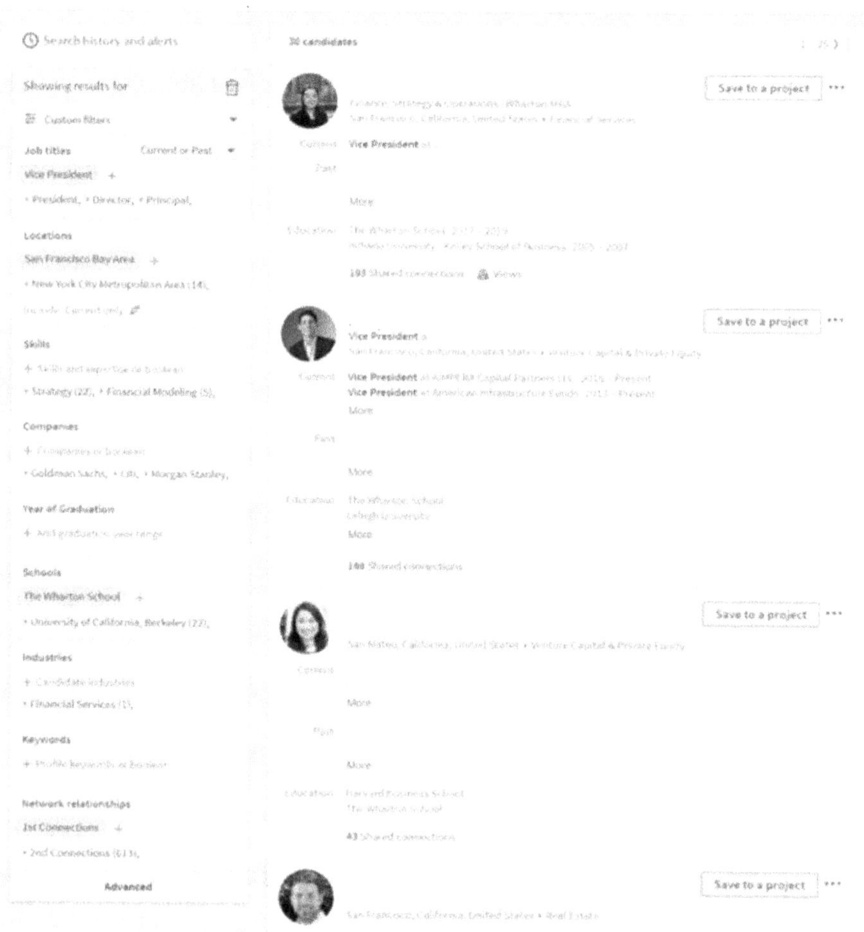

The blue terms on the left are the search criteria the recruiter entered. On the right are the profiles that match.

When a profile is selected, this is the profile that is displayed. Notice how different it is from the “public” LinkedIn profiles you saw earlier. Below is the same person, but notice how different the LinkedIn Recruiter presentation is versus the public view.

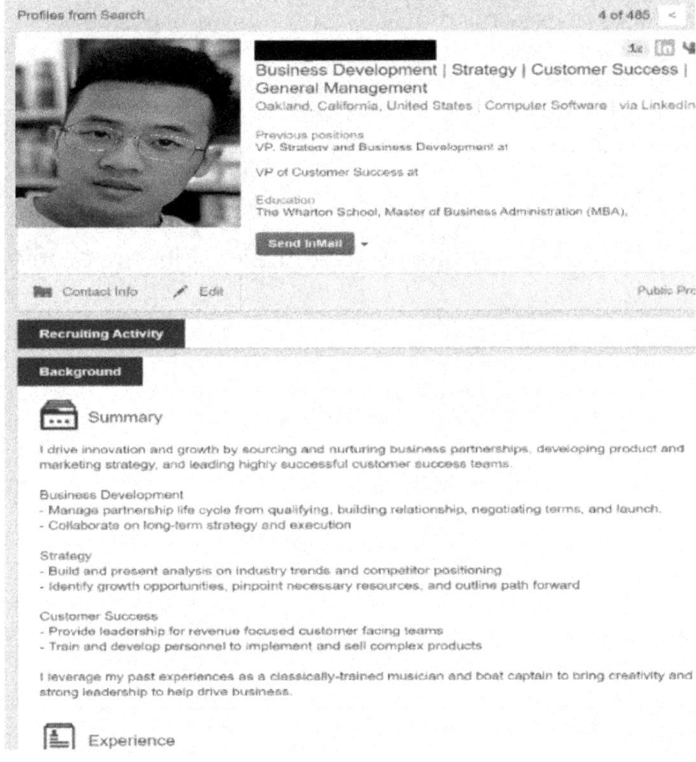

For recruiters, the About section is titled "Summary." We aren't sure why.

Building a Strong LinkedIn Profile

Here's a breakdown of the LinkedIn sections:

- Headline
- About
- Experience
- Education
- Licenses and certifications
- Volunteer experience

- Skills and endorsements
- Recommendations
- Accomplishments
- Interests

We commonly see people update their LinkedIn profile in this order:

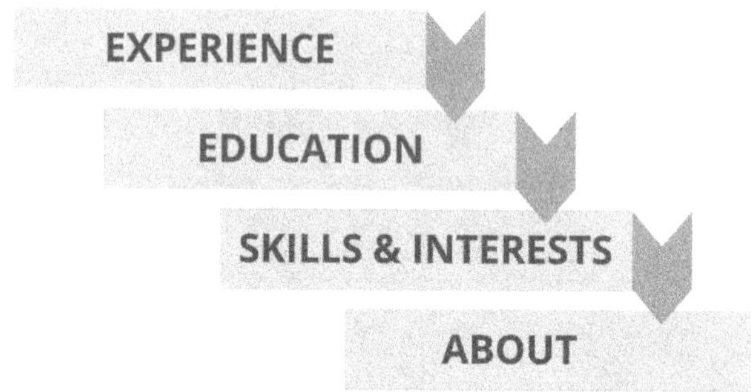

The Typical LinkedIn Profile Writing Process

People usually begin by writing their experiences and wait until the end to edit the About section. We'd suggest an approach like this instead:

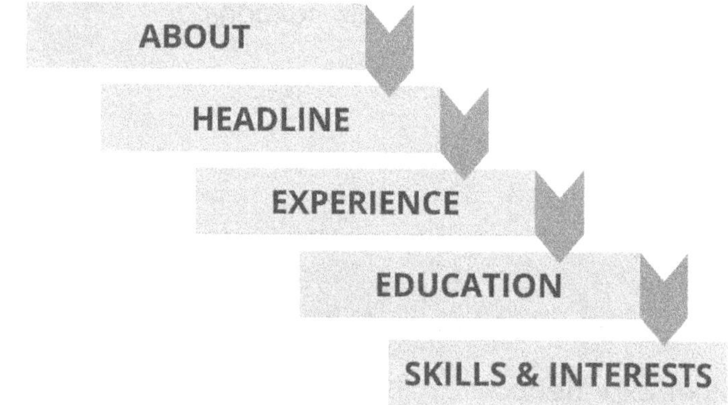

The JOB SEARCH *Manifesto*'s LinkedIn Writing Model

Most clients we work with find the About section intimidating. As a result, they rush through it, writing a bare-bones summary that isn't helpful to recruiters.

If the About section intimidates you, we have good news: you've already written much of it in the exercises from earlier sections of this book. To craft the About section, you simply modify your brand statement and combine it with the accomplishments you've identified in the process of making it.

The **JOB SEARCH** *Manifesto*'s LinkedIn About section model includes:

- a summary based on an edited brand statement
- experience subsections
- accomplishments in a bulleted or narrative format

Here are three examples using one or more of these elements:

The "About" Section Writing Model

In the About section, the brand statement becomes more like a summary. Since you'll be talking about your accomplishments later, you should omit any from your modified brand statement.

As a reminder of what a brand statement looks like, here are some of the examples we shared earlier.

LinkedIn "About" Section Brand Statements

In the examples below, we've highlighted the brand statement but have also included accomplishments or experiences.

I bring extensive experience as Product and Technology Leader in building multimillion dollar B2B and B2C products from inception to launch while managing/mentoring global

Innovator:

- I am customer obsessed. Rather building products from business goals, I thrive building products for consumers and aligning user goals with business goals. This vision helped me build successful product features and design B2C products such as <company name> (100+ Million users) and <company name> for $2 Million + users.
- Won MVP award early in my career for competing and building the most innovative product across the company; success attributed to my understanding of SMB consumers.
- Moved B2B with Business Intelligence analytics product which became a top product with $400+ M revenues and 1M + users. Forged trust relation among top accounts of the product, increasing retention and driving usage. Received Product Excellence Award, granted many customer care awards from customers.

Deep Technical Skills:

- Bridge person: The ability to speak both business and technical language helped me bridge gap between business, marketing, and engineering teams.

- So be it building real-time data visualization and prediction, adding scalable cloud architecture to reduce latency and serve global users or recognizing the need for SEAMLESS SAML authentication to increase activation and usage with top customers – all these features envisioned with my technical expertise in big data analysis, predictive analysis, end to end Web development, IAM etc.

Global Leadership to Deliver Products:

- Hired, managed and mentored high performing product/ engineering teams in UK, Canada, India, Europe and United States. Led many (15+) cross-functional teams at a time through successful product release cycles.
- Introduced and incorporated Agile Scrum, Kanban, extreme programming, and Lean development to improve software delivery/development.

What I can do . . .

As an entrepreneur, I have led the formation and implementation of entrepreneurial ventures in FinTech, real estate, import/export, water, a nonprofit, and most recently a member-owned innovation ecosystem known as FinTech portfolio. I am capable of going from idea to business/ product launch with limited resources to test hypotheses and business models.

As a business developer, I can implement online and offline marketing strategies to develop new relationships and generate revenue for early stage companies (B2C and B2B). Experienced building and managing relationships with high-net-worth individuals, C-Level execs, entrepreneurs, traders, portfolio managers, customers, partners, job candidates, advisors, vendors, internal and external service providers, and regulators. Previous business development experience gained in B2C and B2B settings in various company stages.

As a business manager, I drive strategic initiatives for asset managers focused on business integration, financial system implementations, regulatory oversight, and risk management. I am an expert in portfolio risk analytics, P&L, attribution, operations, and trade life-cycle management for multi-asset class portfolios.

As a business and technically savvy leader, I can translate business requirements into an IT strategy and road map and manage prioritization, execution, and relationships to get the job done. I excel in business analysis and product management roles in fintech, trading, analytics and risk management systems (Calypso, Summit, Aladdin), and fixed income. By combining in-depth knowledge of sophisticated risk analytics and investment systems with capital markets and business process expertise, I can lead initiatives to tackle a variety of risk management and business process challenges.

I help organizations mature, evolve, transform.

I'm an empathetic and transformative leader with a unique blend of strategy, operations, and change management experience that spans more than 20 years.

I've driven business strategies, large change initiatives, and end-to-end process improvements across many key functions in big industries, including consumer packaged goods, health care, and technology.

My approach is methodical and process oriented. My results are measurable and clear.

More about me:

- I succeed through strong consulting skills and the ability to influence up and across.
- I thrive in fast-paced environments and work extremely well in ambiguous situations.
- I can navigate large, complex environments.
- I am a strong project manager and an effective change leader.
- Some of my best career moments:
    - incubating robotic process automation capabilities at <company name>
    - bringing shared services to <company name>
- defining a new way of operating for marketing teams across 25 countries at <company name>.
- moving <company name>'s 800-person IT function from San Francisco, CA, to Frederick, MD
- identifying $40 million in operating cost savings for <company name>'s largest business unit and strategy office
- managing the post-merger integration of a commodities brokerage firm at <company name>

A business technology executive with a Wharton MBA and 16 years of success aligning technology to business. I am

passionate about building and mentoring top-performing cross functional teams to solve complex business problems.

Global leader: I am leading a high-performing cross-functional global team of 300+ people comprised of directors, product managers, architects, and developers. Hired, managed, and mentored teams in the US, UK, and India.

Digital Transformation and Change Leader: Transforming business processes and competencies into a strategic competitive advantage by automating delivery capabilities, implementing data analytics, and nurturing a collaborative agile culture resulting in improved speed-to-market, better quality, and optimized cost.

Financial Responsibilities: Experienced in managing P&L for multiple accounts. Currently responsible for multimillion capital and overhead budgets.

Product and Program Management: I have successfully launched multiple products by engaging with customers at business and technology level (two US patents). Experience in commercializing homegrown products to multiple entertainment studios. Knowledge of complex probability models to perform customer base analysis and customer-based corporate valuation.

Business and Technical Knowledge: I have delivered and executed multiple technology strategies helping business achieve their financial goals. I can speak both business and technical language to bridge the gap between business, engineering, infrastructure, and marketing teams. I hold a bachelor's degree in computer science and engineering and have extensive hands-on experience architecting and building multiple B2C and B2B web applications.

Specialties: digital transformation / general management / strategy / negotiation / vendor management / product & program management / customer success

Writing the "About" Section

Your accomplishments and experiences are important parts of your LinkedIn profile. They let recruiters and hiring managers know whether you have the skills necessary to fill the role they are looking for.

But what's the difference between an accomplishment and an experience?

An accomplishment is a specific project or task you've completed that demonstrates your abilities. Here are two examples of accomplishments:

1. Led a cross-functional team that developed an improved procurement process for a manufacturing company, saving them $1.5 million in the first twelve months.

2. Sold an enterprise's first software solution worth $150,000 in a new targeted market.

An experience goes a little broader than an accomplishment. It points to more than one project. With an experience you're looking at something you've done well multiple times throughout your career.

Here are two experience examples:

1. Responsible for customer success relationships with top five clients representing 40 percent of the company's revenue for the past three years.
2. Led all accounting functions during multiple system (accounting, ERP, and CRM) integration over a two-year period.

An experience is more cumulative than an accomplishment. It describes successes you've had over a long period of time. In contrast, an accomplishment is a single significant project that you've completed.

EXERCISE: WRITE YOUR ACCOMPLISHMENTS OR EXPERIENCES

Below, write out some of your accomplishments and/or experiences. As you write these, try to minimize buzzwords and avoid current catchphrases.

While completing the exercise, keep in mind that the About section has a character limit of 2,000. If you need to, go back and edit your work to be less than 2,000 characters after you've finished.

Accomplishments or experience	Description

Writing the Headline

Your LinkedIn headline defaults to your current position. To change it to something more eye catching that allows the reader to quickly understand you, we'd recommend using bullets of key information.

The headline area is small. You only have 120 characters to work with, and you're going to need to leave room between the dividers. Brevity is everything. The best approach is to create one- or two-word "bullets" separated by dividers. We prefer to use lines ("|") as dividers, but some people use commas.

The primary function of the bullets is to synopsize you. If you're not sure what to use, go back over the About section and look for key terms. These may include your job and important traits.

Another approach to crafting your LinkedIn headline is to write a narrative statement that encapsulates your skills and experiences. We're not fans of this format because it's difficult to summarize more than a couple of generic ideas. But if this type of headline is more appealing to you, there are some samples below to get you started.

Below are a few headline examples using the divider format:

Community leader | Connector | Event organizer and planner

Product and engineering leader | strategy | digital transformation

Product management leader | Cloud applications strategy & launch |

MBA

Writer, editor, content strategist

These headlines work well because they're concise and give the reader an idea of what will follow in the "About" and "Experience" sections.

Here are several headlines that use narrative format:

Entrepreneurial & passionate sales leader seasoned in consultative & relationship partnerships

Global technology marketing leader helping businesses launch disruptive products & services, think global, and give back

Helping companies scale HR, legal, and business operations

Senior leader with extensive experience in corporate finance and operations

Narrative headlines tend to be generic and less direct, but there is no right or wrong method. The choice is yours and should be based on what you feel is the best way to describe yourself.

EXERCISE: WRITE YOUT LINKEDIN HEADLINE

The exercise below includes space for you to write headlines using bullet points and narrative format in case you want to compare them, but you don't have to do both.

Bullet points	
Narrative	

The "Experience" Section

If you wrote a compelling About section, this is where the reader will come next. The Experience section is meant to validate and add more detail to your statements in your About section.

Marketing Leader Example

- Responsible for developing and executing the US digital marketing strategies for franchise, product, and pipeline teams in <company name> business unit, ensuring timely execution with key performance indicators met or exceeded, managing budgets totaling $4 million annually, and overseeing 16 external partner vendors/agencies.

- Launched 4 new franchise-level website properties, leading large cross-functional teams from concept through market research, design, development, and testing—one of the websites was recognized with an industry award for patient centricity.

- Executed several pilot programs to assess the impact of new technologies, channels, and systems, all of which ultimately informed commercial guidance for the organization.

- Lead development of a first-ever integrated customer relationship program for a <company division> product that was recognized with a marketing excellence award for innovation and customer focus.

- Helped to build and launch an empowered partnership framework, as part of a special project team, to improve quality and effectiveness of partnership across commercial channel.

- Applied expertise through volunteer community involvement—taproot foundation.

Sales Leader Example

- Managed accounts exceeding $240 million in revenue, overseeing 10 sales representatives.
- Broadened product distribution by establishing effective relationships with channel partners.
- Reduced customers' complaints by 24 percent via new daily order entry check mark for sales representatives.
- Successfully helped strategic accounts to increase sales 18 percent by working closely with distributors on final price formulation and end-user prospecting.
- Led channel strategy project, developing 6 new channel accounts in strategic regions where company did not have distribution coverage.

Human Resources Example

- Sole HR leader to 6 sites throughout Northern California to 450 employees within the finance, sales, distribution, and supply chain business units.
- Provide strategic partnership with all levels within business units to set people strategies and solve business challenges. Coach managers and staff in effective conflict resolution and mediation, risk management, and effective leadership, increasing employee engagement and decreasing investigations and grievances by 85 percent.

- Consult with senior leaders to assess, plan, and implement leadership classes focused on building leadership skills to support business strategy and objectives; end-to-end ownership, development, and facilitation resulting in 13 percent bench strength growth.

- Meet with staff to discuss operational/managerial opportunities and plant-wide initiatives, increasing engagement by 6 percent.

- Manage employee and labor relations, perform employee complaint and policy-violation investigations, and built relationship with shop stewards, deescalating employee issues by 85 percent.

Sales Account Manager Example

- Provider of enterprise IT database management software.
- President's Club and 130 percent quota attainment.
- Pioneered new software sales divisions and responsible for 30 percent growth in product sales.
- Collaborated with product management, product marketing, and strategic IT partners to create promotions and drive product direction and sales.
- Responsible for selling to Fortune 100 to start-up companies.

Military Leader Example

The 160th special operations aviation regiment's mission is to organize, equip, train, resource, and employ army special operations aviation forces worldwide in support of contingency missions and combatant commanders.

Known as night stalkers, these soldiers are recognized for their proficiency in nighttime operations. They are highly trained and ready to accomplish the very toughest missions in all environments, anywhere in the world, day or night, with unparalleled precision. They employ highly modified Chinook, Black Hawk, and assault and attack configurations of Little Bird helicopters.

- VP of operations (ops-o) for a special mission organization comprised of 5 companies, 611 soldiers, and 26 helicopters valued at $900 million.
- Principle advisor to the chief operations officer (s3) on soldier combat readiness, unit training management (UTM), and the tactical employment of the force's $20.3 million annual budget.
- Prepared, managed, and executed the chief executive officer's (commander's) annual training guidance for the 5,700 flying hour program valued at over $14 million.
- Provided deliberate and contingency aviation support to regional task forces and theater commanders specializing in the central and Pacific regions (Centcom and PACOM).
- COO (s3) for a deployed aviation task force of 152 soldiers. Synchronized precision rotary wing and unmanned aerial systems (UAS) support to joint combat forces.

EXERCISE: WRITE YOUR ACCOMPLISHMENTS

List several accomplishments in your career. First focus on the type of accomplishment it is: you fixed, improved, or created a product or solution. Then write a brief summary. Ideally it is two sentences, three at the most.

Type	Summary
Fixed Improved Created	
Fixed Improved Created	
Fixed Improved Created	
Fixed Improved Created	

This is the area that will closely interface with your résumé. For now, we want you to focus on identifying your accomplishments. When we get to your résumé, we're going to sharpen your accomplishments. But given the amount of content you need to create for LinkedIn, this will give you a strong start.

"Education" Section

Usually people provide just the bare minimum information in their Education section: school attendance dates and degree. That info is helpful, but you can add much more. Consider these areas:

- Group projects (both formal and side projects)—describe them and the results;
- Travel experiences—not just where you went but what you saw and learned;
- Did you apply classroom experience to a real-world project or idea?

Below are some sample Education sections:

University of California, Los Angeles
Bachelor of Arts (B.A.), History

Activities and Societies: Alpha Gamma Delta, Dance Marathon, UCLA Swim Club, AAP, UCLA Rho Lambda Women's Honor Society, UCLA Gamma Sigma Alpha Greek Honor Society, Project Literacy, ECPHP at the Semel Institute of Neuroscience, California Teach

Seattle University
B.P.A, Public Administration

Activities and Societies: Student Body President, Energy Conservation Task Force Director, President of Alpha Sigma Nu--National Jesuit Honor Society, Graduate of Seattle University Honors Program focusing on liberal arts and the Great Books of western civilization.

Completed Bachelor of Public Administration degree (magna cum laude), completed University's Honors Program of humanities, served as student body president, member of Alpha Sigma Nu, National Jesuit Honor Society.

Chabot College
Passive and Active Solar Architecture and Construction Techniques

University of Pennsylvania - The Wharton School
Master of Business Administration (MBA)

Activities and Societies: President of consulting club, member of tech club, and initiated tech coaching sessions for peers.

* Team selected from Wharton Global Consulting practice to define go to market strategy for Palo Alto Network's commercial segment. Defined market size and presented go-to-market recommendations (with reorganization of their sales model) to achieve growth up to $2 billion. Received accolades from client.

* Selected by Illuminate Venture—out of hundreds of internship candidates—to assess the usefulness and market value of a UTM security product architected by former Symantec employees. Made successful case for funding decision.

EXERCISE: Deepen Your Education Section

Document your academic experiences in the three categories we discussed: academic projects/awards, groups you belonged to, and other significant experience.

Academic projects and/or awards	
Groups	
Significant experience	

Headshots

When it comes to headshots, more is less. Get a headshot that's appropriate to your industry and role. Here are some headshot best practices for your LinkedIn profile:

- A smile goes a long way, but don't overdo it. Aim for a warm expression that feels comfortable and looks natural.
- Your face should take up roughly 80 percent of the picture.
- Wear clothes that would match what you would wear in a business setting.
- A professional headshot is best. If you're not sure where to get one, go on Yelp and search "headshot photographers."
- Don't use your driver's license or any other picture that includes a lot of personal information.
- Do not use a group photo. The focus of your LinkedIn headshot should be you.

Examples of good headshots

Source: dreamstime.com

Examples of not so good headshots

	This outfit is too casual. Wearing sunglasses is a no-no. In the photo, we have no sense of the person because the sunglasses mask the eyes and her real facial expression.
	There are several reasons why this headshot doesn't work. First, her profile is only 20 to 30 percent of the total picture. The light is behind her, shining into the upper part of the picture. Finally, the image is blurry.
	Humorous pictures are always big fails. Emphasize who you are, but don't try to perform or be humorous. Your goal is to be genuine. *Source: dreamstime.com*

Your LinkedIn headshot will measure 400 x 400 pixels. If the photo is larger, LinkedIn will shrink it and let you choose how it's framed. If the photo is large, you may need to decrease the size with a photo editor before posting it.

Background Pictures

Your background picture on LinkedIn can help demonstrate who you are and what you are passionate about.

Don't settle for the default background. Choose something that reflects your interests or experiences. The image doesn't have to be literal. There's nothing wrong with choosing something that's a bit abstract.

Here are some categories to consider:

- leadership
- sales
- finance
- operations
- health and wellness

To make sure the key parts of your background photo don't overlap with your headshot, concentrate them on the right side. The LinkedIn background image size is 1584 x 396.

Two resources for free background graphics are Canva and Unsplash. Canva has both free and subscription services. If you want to add text or have a more involved image, you can create it there. Unsplash is a free photo and image site; you'll find lots of choices and ideas there.

> "By combining the work on my brand statement with the keyword search realities of LinkedIn, I now get solicitations from recruiters with jobs that actually interest me. Before, I'd get pinged for roles from my previous career."
>
> **Daniel A. Chen**

Summary

We have strong feelings about your LinkedIn profile: it is more important than a résumé. It's why this is one of the most important chapters in the book. We have covered a lot of ground.

- Recruiters have a special tool called LinkedIn Recruiter that has a unique view of your profile. It emphasizes the top of your profile.
- The About section of your LinkedIn profile is the most important part of your profile. Put your biggest effort here.
- Your Experience section should validate your About section.
- Metrics are important in both the About and Experience sections.
- Your headline needs to be more than the title of your current role. It should highlight your accomplishments and/or superpowers.
- Your headshot needs to be a good representation of your professional experience.
- Canva and Unsplash are two sites you can use to find or create a background image.

THE RÉSUMÉ

Manifesto

- A résumé is not a chronology of your entire work history; it's a marketing document.
- A résumé is targeted for specific roles or opportunities.
- The first step in a job search should never be to update your résumé.
- If you ask five people for résumé feedback, you will get ten opinions.

Gary: His Updated Résumé Told the Right Story

When Gary began working with Steve, he was a technical leader in the telecommunications industry who wanted to change his career direction to strategy and consulting. Gary arrived at their first coaching session with a rambling three-page résumé, wondering how they could "add" strategy to it.

Steve reviewed the résumé with Gary, noting it had no references to strategy. The résumé described the functional details of each of Gary's jobs, but there was little about his impact or accomplishments. They would need to do more than "add."

Since Gary was interested in strategy and consulting, the initial coaching work helped Gary craft a brand statement that emphasized his experiences and accomplishments that were relevant to these areas.

Gary's résumé tied his experience as a technical leader to his skill with analytics and problem-solving. Along with emphasizing skills and accomplishments that were relevant to strategy and consulting, as they had in Gary's brand statement, they worked on putting this information concisely.

Finally, Gary used his coaching sessions to create a strategy-focused résumé template that could be updated as his career progressed. When it was done, Gary's résumé was one succinct page. Shortly after, he found a job with a major consulting firm.

Several years later, Gary reconnected with Steve. This time, Gary wanted to move into senior leadership. Combining his experience with technical management and his recent strategy successes increased Gary's résumé to two pages, but this was necessary due to his increased range of experience.

When Gary met with Steve to work on the updated résumé, he brought his old three-page résumé along with the edited version they'd created the last time they'd worked together. Placing the documents side by side, Gary told Steve that they looked like they were for two different people. And they were.

About This Chapter

Résumés are important, but not as important as they were in the past. Because of the prevalence of one-click applying, résumés are easier to send out than they used to be. Nowadays, résumés are usually scanned and sent online before being filtered with the help of application tracking systems.

Still, having a clear, current résumé is necessary for the following situations:

- when applying to a job application online
- when it's necessary to provide one to a contact before an informational interview
- when you're on your way to an on-site interview; if you're meeting with multiple people, bring one copy for each person you'll be meeting with, along with one or two extras.

Your résumé is a marketing document targeting a specific role and/or opportunity in a company. A focused, well-written résumé should reinforce your brand statement and center on the impact you've had in your career.

When you write your résumé, you should not simply detail your entire work history and education. Recruiters can view that on LinkedIn.

Job seekers frequently start their search by editing their résumé. This is almost always the wrong place to start. Most of our clients who begin this way become frustrated with their lack of progress, and we must start their search over from scratch.

Before crafting your résumé, you should have a clear sense of what roles, organizations, and industry you're targeting. You also need to know how to relate these to your career accomplishments. How can you write a résumé without knowing the roles you want or the audience who will read it?

Several years ago, one of Mike's friends was talking to him about the difficulty of getting feedback on his résumé. He summed it up this way: "I asked five people and received ten opinions!"

We'll focus this chapter on the structure of a résumé, pulling pieces from other chapters in the book. Then we'll use three steps to create high-impact, easy-to-read résumés.

Résumé Structure

To keep a résumé tight and effective, we use four sections as the base résumé structure. The pyramid diagram below shows the sections. Each section reinforces and elaborates on the section above it.

There are lots of formats and structures for résumés floating around, but we prefer chronological résumés. They are the most expected format and frankly are easier to read. As recruiters, each of us reads dozens and dozens of résumés daily. Chronological résumés make it easy to understand a candidate's total background.

There are also lots of creative résumé templates. One word of caution: many applicant tracking systems have trouble "reading" them.

There's also a lot of discussion about using one-page versus two-page résumés. This depends more on your experience and years of work. Here's a rough guideline: If you've worked at more than five roles in your career, you'll probably have three to five key accomplishments per role. That will push you close to two pages, especially if you have a long Education section. There's nothing wrong with two pages if each page is crisp, effective, and speaks directly to the needs of the role and organization.

The Four Parts of a Résumé

The four sections of a résumé are:

- brand title
- brand statement
- work history and job scope
- key accomplishments and impact

Let's explain each section in more detail and start to create your own sections.

Brand Title

We're clear on this: It's the job title or a very succinct summary of your applicable skills for the role you're interested in. The brand title sets the stage for the content that follows. It can be based on your LinkedIn headline, except it should be briefer. Below are some examples:

Product Manager

Sales and Business Development

Experienced Go-To Market Leader

Accountant in Manufacturing

The sample brand titles are very targeted and are meant to show alignment with the job you're interested in. The brand title encourages the reader to learn more about the job seeker. Additionally, you are making it easy for a reader to immediately understand your job search focus.

If you are applying to jobs in several categories, the brand title needs to be adjusted for each category. As an example, if you're applying for both sales and marketing roles, you'll need a different brand title for each.

EXERCISE: WRITE YOUR BRAND TITLE

Write out a brand title that is focused on the category or position in which you are interested.

Brand Statement

This is another key area where you'll again use your brand statement. You can "import" the first paragraph from your LinkedIn profile, though you'll be abbreviating and adjusting it. Keep it to no more than three lines. With a smaller word count, you must avoid passive words or filler words that dilute your message. The words need to show your impact right up front.

We've complied a long list of résumé and LinkedIn impact words. You'll find them in the appendix at the end of this book.

EXERCISE: WRITE YOUR RÉSUMÉ BRAND STATEMENT

Write out an abbreviated form of your brand statement.

Work History and Job Scope

This is the essential information that shows the reader your career progression and accomplishments—the core information for your career. There are four required information pieces:

- company name
- location
- employment dates
- job title

Here are some ideas to consider as you write each.

Company name.

For lesser-known companies, or if you worked for a division of a larger company, you may want to add a summary of the company's service, product, or niche. This summary needs to be brief, ideally no more than two sentences.

If you're no longer at the organization and need to provide an explanation, check out their website. Use some of the site info to craft the summary. Again, keep it brief.

Location

For North American résumés, unless the location is not a major city, you don't need to list the state. Outside of your country, indicating the city and country is a must. Below is an example.

Company X	*March 2016–Present*
Operations Manager	Teaneck, New Jersey

Key Accomplishments and Impact

This is the core part of your résumé: the accomplishments that you list for each job in your career. For your résumé, we're going to use the accomplishments you wrote in the LinkedIn section. But we're going to be more succinct and action oriented.

When you write your accomplishments in your résumé, they should speak directly to the needs of the company and role you are applying for. They typically belong to one of three categories. We use the acronym FIC for fixed, improved, or created.

Fixed. How you repaired a preexisting problem or issue that barely worked or didn't work. Explain how you solved it and the results.

EXAMPLE: Streamlined the customer onboarding process that was taking almost two weeks down to three business days.

Improved. You significantly improving a functional product or process. Explain the before, the after, and the improvements.

EXAMPLE: Reorganized a struggling North American business unit by revamping organizational structure and elevating strong leaders. Revenue grew 25 percent in the following six months.

Created. You were on a team that built a solution or product from scratch. Explain what you created and the impact.

EXAMPLE: Built a custom reporting solution for our largest customer from scratch, which was later added to the main product.

Typically, résumés use the four-step STAR model: situation, tactics, action, and results. As you document these accomplishments, use the SAR model (situation, action, and result). The fundamental reason for a résumé is to be a marketing document that invites a conversation about your career. Detailing tactics in a success story is useful in an interview but is too much information for a résumé. Here are some examples.

STAR: "Redefined and launched new go-to-market strategies by creating four working groups to change outdated strategies. This increased annual global revenue 84 percent in the first year."

SAR: “Redefined and launched new go-to-market strategies that increased annual global revenue 84 percent in the first year.”

In the STAR example, the phrase “by creating four working groups to change outdated strategies” adds too much detail. It obscures the first-year results. The STAR model explains that the situation is the existence of outdated go-to-market strategies. In the SAR model, the situation is implied: the existing go-to-market strategies weren’t effective.

The SAR result has both brevity and impact. It gets right to the point, quickly showing the results: 84 percent the first year. It provides bigger impact in fewer words.

- Describe situations: problems, stakeholders, tension, business challenges, and timelines.
- Describe your actions: analysis, strategy, process improvement, implementation/execution, restructuring, influence, negotiation, innovative approach, and new ideas.
- Describe your results: revenue impact, cost savings, customer growth, scaling, team growth/development. Make sure to quantify using data points.

Below are a few examples:

- Brought in to grow <company>’s therapy business following the acquisition of a German-based technology company.
- Launched hypothesis-driven growth initiative to identify the future diversification strategy anticipating the changing mobile marketplace.

EXERCISE: WRITE A SAR

Select one of your FIC examples (fix, improve, or create) and build out an experience bullet point for your résumé.

Situation	
Action	
Result	
Résumé bullet point	

Writing about Metrics

Often, adding metrics to success stories is a challenge. In every story there's a metric that increases the impact. To make it easier, success metrics usually come in three categories: time, volume, and money.

Think about the *time* your success story saved. Another time metric is the number of months, days, or hours a person or team focused on a deliverable. Below are a few examples:

- "Saved our marketing team over 200 hours a month by improving the approval process."
- "Our team invested over 500 hours to deliver a detailed financial model."

Consider *volume* metrics such as units made, number of tasks, or projects. Another volume metric is hiring and growing a team. Below are some examples:

- "Consistently closed over 500 customer tickets a month, an increase of 60 percent above team average."
- "Improved quality control resulted in 50 percent less product returns."
- "Doubled team size from 6 to 12"

It's easy to focus on *money* made or revenue. But also think about money saved, as in these examples:

- "New product generated $1 million in the first six months."
- "New process saved over $100,000 in the first year."

Remember, you can also *combine metrics* that increase the power of your success story. It's common to include a volume statement after a time or money metric. This shows how quickly your success story had impact with the speed it was implemented. Also, money metrics have greater impact when a time metric is included. Below are some examples:

- "Increased customer base by 45 percent in less than 9 months by simplifying the sales process."
- "Shipped over 2,500 units in the first month of product release, resulting in an almost 50 percent growth in sales."

Résumé Formatting

Three areas often confuse people when they're writing their résumé: number of pages, number of bullets per job, and writing for ATSs.

Number of Pages

We're asked a lot about what is an appropriate number of pages in a résumé. Remember, your résumé is a marketing document, not a complete job history. You want to make it focused and easy to follow.

As a rule of thumb, if you have less than a decade of experience, or three or fewer roles, build a one-page résumé. But never go beyond two pages because then your core message and emphasis will become too hard to follow.

Number of Bullets per Job

The number of bullets are not just based on the experience but how relevant they are to the role. Five bullets per role is the maximum, but which roles do you emphasize? Ideally those that are the most recent. Usually, the further back a role is, the fewer bullets you use. But if past experiences are relevant, include them. The content of your résumé is more important than the format.

Writing a Résumé for Applicant Tracking Systems

This is an easy answer: don't do it. As former recruiting leaders, we've implemented multiple ATSs. They are designed to speed up the processing of candidate reviews but also to streamline the interviewing and hiring process.

ATSs do not decide whether a candidate is qualified—a human recruiter makes that determination. At most, an ATS might "grade" candidates, but nothing more.

Don't create a "word salad" of keywords. Write clearly and explain how your experience is a solid match for the role. A human will read it and make the decision.

Summary

Success stories that clearly show you can do the job you're applying for should be the core of your résumé. The goal is to trigger interest and start a dialogue about you and the role.

- Your résumé is constructed with four components: (1) brand title, (2) brand statement, (3) work history and job scope, and (4) key accomplishments and impact.
- Use the FIC model to identify success stories. What did you fix, improve, or create?
- Organize and write success stories using the SAR model: situation, action, and results.
- Include metrics and consider describing time, volume, or money made or saved.
- Your résumé should be no longer than two pages and only one page if you have less than a decade of work experience.
- Keep the number of bullets for each job between three and five, with more bullets for the most recent jobs.
- Write your résumé for a human to read, not an applicant tracking system.
- With your stories in place, a compelling LinkedIn profile, and a solid action plan, it's time to execute your job search.

JOB SEARCH EXECUTION

Manifesto

- A job search is a multidimensional process.
- Just sending in a résumé for a job post is like cold-calling: the success rate is low.
- Always research and find internal advocates first.

Mark's Multidimensional Job Search

Mark was a senior finance leader with prior experience in investment banking and recent experience leading and growing finance teams for start-ups. He felt ready to take the next step in his career. His aspiration was to be chief financial officer (CFO) at a later-stage start-up company with potential liquidity events or exit, such as a merger and acquisition (M&A) or going public through an initial public offering (IPO).

His background was substantial; he had experience building and growing start-up finance teams mostly at fast-growing start-up companies. The only thing missing from his background was leading companies through an exit. This was experience that would almost certainly be required.

For most of his target opportunities, the companies were seeking CFOs with a track record of financial leadership through IPO or M&A. Mark had never successfully taken a company through an exit but did have substantial M&A and some IPO experience in a prior job as an investment banker.

For Mark to land a CFO role, he would need the help of a strong network and internal connections. This was the core problem: Mark was pursuing opportunities by just applying to online postings. He got few responses, and Mark became discouraged. Unfortunately, the recipients of his applications were either not seeing or not appreciating his banking experience as relevant. Mark reached out to us for coaching to solve this problem.

The coaching process started by creating a clear but comprehensive brand statement using *The Job Search Manifesto* brand statement model. Since Mark knew his audience, he also updated his LinkedIn profile and résumé with the same points from his brand statement.

His LinkedIn profile, résumé, and verbal introduction all synced up around three main messages:

- Mark is an aspiring CFO with success building and scaling start-up finance teams.
- He has led finance strategy, operations, partnerships, investments, and accounting.
- He has prior investment banking portfolio experience with technology company M&As and IPOs.

With a unified message, Mark's next coaching steps put it all together: his application tactics were altered.

Instead of just applying for roles, Mark also connected directly with CEOs/founders or investors/board members at companies that had posted a job or were quietly doing CFO searches. He found out about the quiet searches through deepening his business relationships and his overall network. Mark shared his brand statement, articulating why he'd be the best financial leader to move their company to the next level.

He also sought out connections for each role at the target companies he applied to, even when he didn't have a direct connection. Many of the reach-outs were fellow alums or friends of friends.

Mark saw his response rate and first-round interview invites increase substantially in just a couple of weeks. His job search pace rose dramatically.

Within weeks of his uptick, he had multiple interviews. Mark found himself deciding between two offers: one for a series C pre-IPO start-up and the other for a series A early-stage start-up. (These series refer to different funding rounds for outside investment.) He accepted the series C CFO role and is now thriving.

About This Chapter

Mark followed much of *The Job Search Manifesto* model, but it all came together when he added another type of outreach: reaching out for a specific role. Successful job searches are built on a thoughtful process of reaching out about jobs and opportunities.

We've repeatedly stated it throughout this book: just sending your résumé and applying is not enough. In fact, simply sending applications is really a crapshoot. Unless you *really* match the role and state that clearly in your résumé, the odds are stacked against you.

We also recognize that job search execution is an iterative process. You will learn a lot at each step and must adjust your methods continually. And that's the goal, to start applying the ideas that we've shared so far and get good at executing.

Mark used coaching to develop an execution plan based on proven methods we've shared for years. The plan involves more work than just sending in a résumé, but, very simply, it works.

Role-Specific Reach-Outs

We introduced the three relationship building tracks in the relationship building chapter. In that chapter we wanted to get you comfortable with the concept of general reaching out, both generic and specific to gaining business knowledge. Those were the "touch" and "explore" tracks.

In this chapter we focus on the third reach-out track, "role-specific." This chapter answers the question of how to do reach-outs for a specific role or an organization you are strongly interested in joining.

We'll share sample role-specific reach-out emails for strong, weak, and dormant ties. Each reach-out is a little bit different, and we want you to note the changes in each.

Also, *The Job Search Manifesto* process involves you working down a reach-out list. You start with the hiring manager or a senior leader to make initial contact, but if you get no response, work your way down, ultimately ending up with a reach-out to a recruiter.

Targeted Outreach—Strong and Weak Ties

When you're looking for a new job, this is where robust and solid business relationships are key. As we noted in the chapter on building business relationships, "weak ties" are key to helping you land your next role. We detailed a structure to develop, maintain, and nurture these relationships. In this phase of a job search, you're going to reach out but with a focused message: there is a job you are interested in. But we want to reinforce another key point: this is *not* networking.

The ideal situation is having strong or weak ties in the organization, but this outreach can sometimes feel awkward—a one-sided transaction. In reaching out about a role, don't make this just about getting the other person to refer you. You also want ideas, guidance, and direction about the company and the role. These people are also likely to give you an unvarnished view of the organization that you might not get from a recruiter or hiring manager.

As we explain in the relationship building chapter, many companies pay a reward or "referral bonus" to their employees when the company hires their referral. The cost of recruiting is high, and referrals are an easy and fast way to hire good people. Asking someone specifically about the role is not an imposition or burden, especially when done tactfully.

Here are two sample email reach-outs: one for strong ties and the other for weak ties.

Strong tie email:

> "Hi Sarah, I noticed your organization has a position for X that's a great match for my skills and experience. I believe I can add a lot to the organization.

> If you have a few minutes in the next day or so, I'd appreciate a short 15-minute call to briefly discuss the role and your organization. I will flex my schedule to yours; I want to respect your time."

Weak tie email (where you have a mutual connection):

> "Hi Sarah, you and I both know Simon Lewis, and he suggested I reach out. I noticed your organization has a position for X that's a great match for my skills and experience. I believe I can add a lot to the organization.
>
> If you have a few minutes in the next day or so, I'd appreciate a short 15-minute call to briefly discuss the role and your organization. I will flex my schedule to yours; I want to respect your time."

In both cases, the emails are brief with a very short pitch; in fact, the pitch is a single sentence. The second paragraph, the "ask," is almost more detailed than the first paragraph. This is how you show respect for the weak or strong tie, keeping the time commitment short and flexible.

If you are no longer working with your company, it's OK to say, "I'm in transition and want to get your thoughts and ideas." Many of our clients have felt awkward doing this but found that it produced strong results. People naturally want to help others, and it's OK to politely ask for thoughts and ideas.

As for managing the call, you only have fifteen minutes when you speak to your strong or weak tie, and you should spend more time listening than talking. Here's one agenda you can follow:

- Introduction: Thank them for taking the time for the call.
- State the name of the role and why you are interested.
- Talk about how your skills and experiences align with the role.
- Ask about their understanding of the role.
- Ask about the company culture and what they enjoy about working there.
- Ask what next steps they recommend for applying and being considered.
- Thank them and close the call.

This is a lot of information to go over in a fifteen-minute call. But the introduction and the ending of the call should only take two minutes total. Keep your interest and your alignment with the role to about three minutes. The remaining ten minutes, which is two-thirds of the total call time, should be focused on the information they provide. It's about them and the information they share. You are listening more than talking.

You can keep your ask subtle here. At this point they understand you are reaching out to possibly get a referral, but if you don't know them well, that can feel uncomfortable. A good way to ask is something like this: "What next steps do you recommend I take to be considered for this role?"

This gives them the flexibility to simply offer a process without feeling obligated to refer or sponsor you. But it also gives them a nice way to offer it on their own. The goal is to move ahead with getting submitted for the job but also maintaining the relationship you have with this person.

You've effectively moved forward if they choose to submit you, but there are other contacts you can quickly make to seek another advocate if your stronger tie chooses not to be an advocate for you.

At this point you're in a waiting mode. If you've received no response within five to seven working days, reach out to your contact and let them know there's been no action. This can be a subtle reminder just in case they've forgotten to submit your name.

Things gets a little trickier if this goes on for longer than seven working days. The next action steps of the job application best practices may come into play.

The best practices are also the steps you want to follow if your strong or weak tie does not offer to refer you. You'll have to find other advocates.

Job Application Reach-Out List

Either with or without a weak or strong tie referral, you still need to avoid blindly submitting your résumé. That is an absolute last resort. The following steps are a list of contacts (in order of priority) that you want to reach out to about the role.

Never simply apply for a job and wait. Yes, applying for roles is an important part of your job search. But the send, wait, and pray approach is not a valid strategy. We want you to identify and reach out to the following people in the organization before you apply:

1. he hiring manager or other leader
2. the head of recruiting or human resources

3.a staff-level recruitert

The prioritization is based on who would have the most influence to get your application noticed and moved forward. Time and again we've seen people successfully get a job just by taking these reach-out steps.

We're going to take the generic emails we showed earlier and refine them further, depending on the person's role. The contact methods are similar, but the messages are slightly different. Here's the process for each contact.

Hiring Manager or Another Leader Reach-Out

Reason to reach out: They have the most to gain since the role is on their team. Rarely do candidates reach out to a hiring manager, which is surprising. As hiring managers ourselves, we've frequently responded when a candidate contacted us directly.

Sample reach-out email:

> "Hi Keisha, I'm reaching out because of my strong interest in the <position name> role. The key responsibilities align well with my background and experience. I've done some research, and I think you are the hiring manager or have a lot of involvement with the role. I am going to apply but have a couple of questions and was hoping we could connect before I send in my résumé.
>
> If you have a few minutes in the next day or so, I'd appreciate a short 15-minute call to briefly discuss the role and your organization. I will flex my schedule to yours; I want to respect your time."

The Head of Recruiting or Human Resources

Reason to reach out: They want to fill the position and are also interested in deepening the company culture. A candidate who shows strong interest and is a good match for the role often triggers a conversation.

Sample reach-out email:

> "Hi Luis, I'm reaching out because of my strong interest in <position name> role that you recently posted. The key responsibilities align well with my background and experience. I know you are busy recruiting for the role, but I have a couple of questions and was hoping we could connect before I send in my résumé.
>
> If you have a few minutes in the next day or so, I'd appreciate a short 15-minute call to briefly discuss the role and your organization. I will flex my schedule to yours; I want to respect your time."

Staff-Level Recruiter

Reason to reach out: They are on the front lines, and their customer is the hiring manager. They are often very busy, but a well-written reach-out can get a conversation started.

Sample reach-out email:

> "Hi Farah, I'm reaching out because of my strong interest in <position name> role that you are recruiting for. The key responsibilities align well with my background and experience. I know you're looking at a lot candidates, and I want to be sensitive to your time. I am going to apply but

have a couple of questions and was hoping we could connect before I send in my résumé.

If you have a few minutes in the next day or so, I'd appreciate a short 15-minute call to briefly discuss the role and your organization. I will flex my schedule to yours; I want to respect your time."

EXERCISE: WRITE ROLE SPECIFIC REACH-OUT EMAILS FOR EACH PERSON

Write your own unique emails for each of the three tracks (touch, explore, and role-specific) we have discussed in this chapter. Use the examples we shared but make them your own.

Hiring manager or leader	
HR leader	
Staff-level recruiter	

The Three-to-Five Dialogue Principle

As recruiters, for every open position, we wanted three to five viable candidates. Most recruiters follow this idea and know that once they have a solid base of clients, they're highly likely to fill the position. We've kept that same principle and have our coaching clients use it. But we invert it.

During a job search, we want our coaching clients to be in dialogue with three to five people weekly. Start out with mainly touch-track dialogues. This will give you a chance to get comfortable with sharing your brand statement and asking questions about business conditions and the other person's career story.

After a few "touch" conversations (track 1 in the list below), "explore" (track 2) conversations will become easier and more important. Then, "role-specific" conversations (track 3) should be added.

We say three to five dialogues because we want you continually talking, sharing, and learning throughout your job search. The low end, three, is if you are busy in your current life or are seeking a very specialized role. Five is a solid number that essentially has you talking to at least one person a day.

Here are some sample dialogues:

- having a call with a good friend about their career journey (track 1 conversation)
- talking to a former coworker you haven't connected with in a while about their current company (track 2)
- connecting with a local leader in your career space, focusing on how they see upcoming challenges and opportunities (track 2);
- scheduling a call with a recruiter about a role you applied for (track 3);

- having an interview with a hiring manager and/or their team about a role for which you are a candidate (track 3).

With the three-to-five principle, we want you keep the process consistent and growing. As one dialogue ends, add others to stay within the three-to-five range. This will consistently make you stronger in your job search communication and will also reduce the emotional ups and downs.

Job Search Tracking

Once you've started executing your job search, staying organized is essential. Here's a tracking sheet you can use to stay organized and focused. You can use the form below to list out your job search activity or build your own in a spreadsheet.

Name	Organization	Role	Track* (T,E,RS)	Notes	Next steps

* T = touch; E = explore; RS = role-specific.

It's easy to maintain this tracker, which you can copy into an Excel, Google Sheets, or Apple Numbers sheet. One important step is to keep the next steps current and use dates in that column. The dates will help you spot your next action

"It was all about the structured and a methodical process to job search. Some of the key attributes were:

1. Positioning yourself: How do you position yourself with a smaller company when you have the experience from a big company (Big to small and small to big)?

2. Superpowers: This seems straight forward but I found it really hard to pen this down without structured thinking.

3. Brand Statement: The culmination of one's successes, superpowers and domain experience leading to the brand statement, was a perspective that I hadn't thought about and had become the opening statement for every interview.

4. Relationship Building: Relationship building vs. networking, as well as the approach to writing your tie with the hook was very helpful to me. I came across as a person who was specific of the ask.

5. Ultimately it made me realize that the book is written so well that it becomes a bible for not just my immediate search but a playbook for my future searches."

Rashmi Ramesh

Summary

A job search execution plan takes key principles and actions from the chapters on sourcing and relationship building and adds some contact best practices and measurement tools to help move your job search progress forward and generate results.

- Outreach is core to your job search. Do not send in a résumé blindly.
- The third outreach track, role-specific, is slightly different from the relationship building outreach and is focused on a particular job or position.
- You still want to build a relationship, but the request to connect is based on a job you are interested in and that they are looking to fill.
- Effectively use both strong and weak ties to gain information and advocacy for a role in their organization.
- Develop your outreach message to strong ties, weak ties, and direct contacts. It should be unique and has to be a comprehensive message.
- The three-to-five dialogue model has you talking with three to five people a week about roles you are interested in.
- Use the tracking system provided above or another to set your pace and stay focused.

INTERVIEWING

Manifesto

- An interview is not a piano recital or performance; it's a conversation.
- The candidate also has power in an interview.
- Only two areas are being evaluated in an interview—competence and culture fit—with both the candidate and the interviewer assessing each other.

Priya Aligns Her Interview Stories and Gets the Offer

Priya had a strong background in business operations leadership with superpowers developed around:

- creating and executing business operations strategy;
- scaling growth in start-ups, especially related to operations and customer success;
- leading business transformation within larger companies.

Her career goal was to land a job as a director of business operations for a top-tier consumer technology brand. Companies she targeted included Amazon, Walmart, Wayfair, and several others.

Priya had a bachelor's degree in economics and started her career in project management. She initially worked for lesser-known start-ups but had success as a business operations manager at a well-known global consumer goods company.

The foundation was there, but Priya came to coaching with frustration about her interview experiences. She was getting a good amount of interest and going to many first-round recruiter interviews. But her interviewing wasn't advancing her beyond one or two rounds.

Her coaching objective was to understand and build a success strategy to advance to final interview rounds and receive an offer.

Coaching sessions with Priya initially focused on mock interviewing and replaying previous interviews. It became obvious that Priya was delivering one-dimensional answers to interview questions. To achieve interview success, Priya needed to:

- adjust her approach more toward promoting her relevant achievements and experiences;
- drive home her brand as an accomplished business operations director;
- validate and demonstrate that she understood the company's challenges;
- close out her stories and finish the interview with more impact by connecting the dots between her skills, accomplishments, and the company's needs.

To achieve these goals, Priya focused on four areas:

- clearly aligning her brand statement with the unique needs and requirements of the role for which she was interviewing;
- deepening her behavioral interview skills to stay focused on providing solid examples that demonstrated her fit for the role;
- developing and asking strong questions to learn more about challenges, problems, and the job scope of the role in question (asking insightful questions would trigger

more balanced exchanges during the interview and help her stay more conversational);

- summarizing key points during each interview, allowing her to reiterate why she was a strong fit for the role.

Once Priya started injecting these strategies into her storytelling and the overall interview process, she became much more comfortable. She soon found herself moving into third and final rounds for multiple opportunities. Within six weeks of implementing her new interview strategy, she accepted an offer as senior manager of business operations for a global consumer technology device company.

About This Chapter

When people are prepping for interviews, we too often see them at opposite extremes. One extreme is that they wing it. They do little prep, instead assuming their strong communication skills will get them through the entire process.

At the other extreme, we've seen people spend far too much time researching every detail about the organization, and everyone they will come in contact with, and not enough time preparing their strategy for connecting the dots between their experience and the role. We obviously recommend a middle ground.

Up front, know that effective interviewing is all about telling relevant stories full of impact that directly apply to the role, team, and organization you are seeking to join. This takes practice to master—but it's the proven approach to succeeding in interviews.

Let's also simplify the interview process. You are only being evaluated in two areas: competence and team fit. When Priya realized this, it reduced her anxiety and made her preparation much less daunting. She communicated her brand statement and answered interview questions clearly and strongly. When she added thoughtful questions that helped tie her stories and examples back to the core needs of the role, Priya was able to make a powerful case that she was the best candidate for the role.

When broken down into manageable chunks, interviews can be a great way to learn not only about the organization but about yourself and your strengths. People who achieve three to five final-round interviews tend to receive job offers.

This middle ground of researching your targets along with preparing your relevant stories will not happen overnight. In fact, we talked about the three-to-five principle in the last chapter, on job search execution. You will need to do multiple interviews to become solid with your process and your answers. Our experience says it takes three to five interview cycles to learn to effectively deliver this information.

When Mike was an internal recruiting leader, he taught interview training classes for interviewers. His program described a successful candidate this way:

> "The candidate is helpful to others and team oriented. They will be a strong peer and make positive contributions to the company's culture. They have the skills to immediately make a solid contribution and possess the ability to learn and master the role."

Our objective in this chapter is to make you a successful candidate: one who matches the description above.

We simplify the prep work needed both before and during interviews and break down this chapter into three areas:

- logistics: understanding the process, schedule, and participants
- questions: preparing for common questions, both behavioral and process oriented, and developing answers that demonstrate your experience and the impact you can bring;
- follow-up: what information you need after the interview is done and what steps to take.

Logistics and follow-up are usually straightforward but often get lost in the flurry of activity surrounding the interview. Often candidates focus so much on question preparation that they lose sight of these basics.

We also share in detail the three major parts of the interview process. This information includes how to prepare, which questions to ask, and key information to make you successful at each stage.

> A key interviewing strategy I've gained is to go beyond merely stating the answer. I have seen many people ump to answers without understanding the entirely of the question.
>
> **Venkat Sadras**

Interview Logistics

Most interview cycles follow the process in the graphic below:

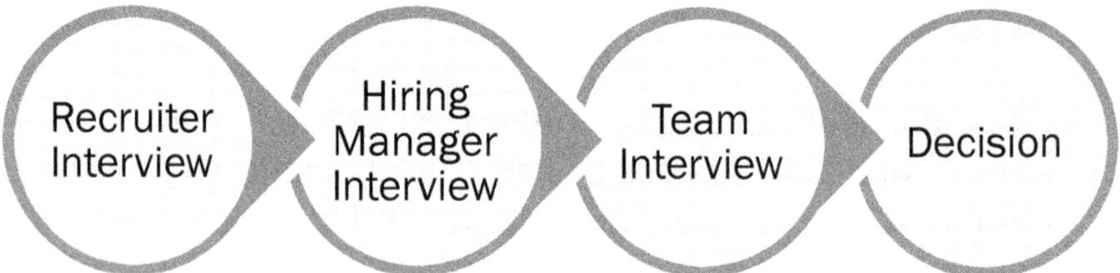

Here's a breakdown of each step and the key objectives.

Each organization is different, and their practices will vary. This is especially true during the pandemic, where almost all hiring is done remotely. We see that companies are now more comfortable with this process, but they want people to weigh in. The result is more people interviewing candidates and the process taking longer than before.

Prepping for interviews has gotten both easier and more complex. Larger organizations often have well-organized interview processes with a set number of interviewers and focused-on topics. Recruiters often provide agendas, key topics, and even questions. They are also likely to provide you the names of the interviewers.

At every step of the interview process, you want to know:

- who will interview you
- what they will focus on
- the start time and the duration of the call

Virtual Interviews

During the COVID-19 pandemic, virtual interviews became the new norm, and preparing for them became both easier and harder than for on-site interviews. Gone were the stressful issues around travel, parking, not getting lost, and arriving on time. And, once in the lobby, looking relaxed and prepared!

But in their place were new concerns about having both technology and a visual environment that supports an uninterrupted video connection that presents you as a solid professional.

We've noticed one area of concern between virtual versus on-site interviews: the length of the interview cycle. Virtual interview cycles are taking longer. Early in the COVID-19 pandemic, organizations initially froze their hiring. They did this for multiple reasons:

- to assess economic conditions and how hiring was affected;
- to allow hiring teams to develop comfort in hiring someone they hadn't met face to face;
- to develop better logistics to handle all remote interview scheduling.

We'll mention this again in this chapter, but candidates need to really understand the time line for the interview process and decision-making. We frequently see clients frustrated with the length of the process. When we've checked, we were told the candidates never asked how long the process would take. Get the time line data early in the interview process. We'll explain when and how shortly.

The issues we've just listed are issues the hiring organizations face. For a candidate, the process should appear clear and straightforward.

> Virtual interviews follow the same approach as in-person interviews except in one case. The types of interviews are:
>
> - one-on-one (1:1)—questions and approaches are the same as in person
> - group or panel—also pretty much the same as an in-person interview
> - prerecorded—this is new, and we'll discuss best practices for the setup and environment

Virtual Interview Setup and Prep

The advantage of a virtual interview is that you're doing it from your workspace—but that's also the disadvantage. The goal of the virtual interview is to have little to no issues related to your setup or environment so you can fully concentrate on the interview dialogue. To ensure that, below is a checklist to follow both before and during a virtual interview.

- **Check the interview link**—Make sure you access the link in advance of the interview. This way any glitches you experience can be corrected by communicating with the organization.

- **Download and test any video conference software needed well in advance**—With the broad range of video conference tools, make sure you've downloaded the app and tested it before the interview. Know how the app works, especially for screen sharing, chat, and the setup icon.

- **Make sure your internet connection is solid**—You want a solid internet connection that clearly transmits your image and voice. If your signal isn't strong, consider moving to a part of your home that is closer to your router. A strong steady signal is key.

- **Be in a quiet place that minimizes background noise and prevents interruptions**—We know this is challenging, especially if you have children in the house, but having a quiet place with the door closed is important.

- **Test your camera and audio**—Make sure the basics of your setup work: your video camera and your microphone. As we mentioned in the point on video conference software, you want to make sure that the microphone and video camera work with the application before the interview.

- **Look into the camera**—Making eye contact in an interview is important and even more so in a virtual interview. Make sure your video camera is at eye level or close to it. This way, making eye contact is easier. Practice this ahead of time.

- **Lighting**—This is often forgotten, but good lighting really helps during a video interview. Lighting isn't about vanity; it's about making sure people can clearly see you and your facial expressions. In most cases a desk lamp situated behind your computer or two desk lamps on either side of you work well. You can also look for different lighting tools on Amazon; many are inexpensive solutions.

- **Dress well (at least your top half)**—Yes, you can wear shorts and sandals! But the top half of what you wear has to be business appropriate. With working from home being the new normal, find out ahead of time what the organization's standard is. Some may insist on standard business wear, such as a blouse and jacket for women and a shirt, jacket, and possibly a tie for men. But more and more organizations are business casual, where a button-down shirt or blouse is sufficient. A simple rule of thumb: wear a blouse or shirt with a collar.

- **Water and refreshments**—Make sure to stock your interview room with enough water and refreshments. This is especially true if you're doing a longer group interview or a series of back-to-back one-on-one interviews. The goal is to be able to stay fresh throughout the process. We don't recommend messy food or full meals—aim for snacks to keep your energy consistent.

- **Bathroom breaks**—Have a plan for this; you want to be comfortable throughout longer interviews. A key to this is muting your microphone and turning off your camera when you leave. Don't just walk out of the room and leave your environment visible and audible.

- **Validate multiple meeting links**—We mentioned links earlier, but if you're interviewing multiple people over multiple days, validate that each link works. Don't assume you'll be using one link through all your virtual interviews.

- **Be mindful of time zone differences**—Teams are more scattered than ever, so you may be talking to people throughout the United States or even worldwide. As you coordinate scheduling, keep this in mind and be flexible. Make sure you respect the interviewer's time, but also don't pack your own schedule. You want to be fresh throughout the process.

- **Optimize your background**—Your background should not distract from you. A simple, well-lit, clean background is ideal. Luckily, many video conference services offer virtual backgrounds. You can use either an interior or exterior image, making sure it frames you well and is not distracting. Several services also offer "background blurring" features. See what works best for you and your environment.

- **You can use notes and browsers**—Learn to use shared-screen features. Never walk into an interview without written-down notes and ideas; this applies to virtual interviews as well. Using browsers and other sources is easier to do in a virtual interview. We suggest you have one or two browser windows open if needed. This doesn't mean you are doing on-the-fly research; instead, you should pull up validating information to support what you already know.

- **Learn to share your screen**—You may want to share your work during an interview, and almost all video conference services provide screen-sharing capabilities. Each one does things differently, so practice before your interview. Ideally you will have ideas about what you want to share and have them loaded and ready before the interview begins.

Prerecorded Virtual Interviews

The idea behind virtual interviews is letting more people in the organization evaluate recorded video interviews. They can be viewed at the hiring team's convenience. While traditionally this has been used for high-volume screening, most often for individual contributor roles, we are seeing this method being used more frequently for management roles.

Services such as Spark Hire, Jobvite, Montage, and HireVue provide these services, and we expect there will be more. These services usually give you a series of base questions to answer. Often they include a brand statement question such as "Tell me about yourself." They usually give you a review step and an approval step. You don't have to submit your first attempt.

Follow the list of best practices we gave you for virtual interviews above, but there is a key step: *eye contact*. Look directly at the camera as you answer the questions.

Recruiter Interviews

In most organizations you will work with one main recruiter throughout the process. An initial recruiter interview is normally just thirty minutes and will cover several areas, including experience validation, culture fit, and a top-level view of the candidate's experience and initial research into the company.

The recruiter's objectives are to:

- learn what the candidate understands about the company and role
- validate that the candidate has experience with many of the role's requirements (notice we didn't say all the requirements)
- provide some marketing and positive information about the organization and team
- get a sense of the candidate's culture fit
- establish a baseline for salary and compensation expectations.

Recruiting Interview Logistics

Interviews are usually just thirty minutes long, so they will not go into deep questions. There are three key preparation areas.

First, research the organization. Read the latest press releases; look up the LinkedIn profile of the recruiter and, if you know them, also the hiring manager.

Second, clearly articulate where your skills and experience align with the job requirements. This is not going to be deep, and don't plan to debate. If you don't possess a key skill, don't overplay or underplay it: acknowledge that the experience or skill isn't in place, but show that other skills you have will let you contribute immediately.

Third, don't fall into the trap of saying "I'm a fast learner." As recruiters, we always took this to mean that before a candidate could really do the job, we would have to train them. In many cases, we knew the organization needed help right away and had little, if any, "ramp" time. (More on this later.) A better answer is: "I can contribute right away, and I also learn quickly."

Recruiting Interview Question Prep

"Tell me about yourself" is a common question you are all set to answer with the brand statement you prepared earlier. As you share your brand statement, point out similarities between your superpowers, domain expertise, or experience and the role. Don't go deep, but an extra comment can show your fitness for the role and organization.

"What are your salary expectations?" This question obviously sets the stage for offer negotiation, but it's important to not dive into negotiations at this stage. You definitely want to understand their range and also establish your salary boundaries.

Multiple states and counties have laws stating that employers can't ask for an applicant's pay and salary history. Some states such California and Washington require employers to provide salary and pay information upon a candidate's request.

Paycor has a page on their site focused on tracking salary disclosure laws: https://www.paycor.com/resource-center/states-with-salary-history-bans (15).

Never give one number; always provide a range. The low-end number should be your minimally acceptable number, ideally higher than your current salary or pay. The top end should be based on research you do using sites such as Glassdoor, Comparably, or Salary.com. Remember, you are only quoting a range, *not* getting into a negotiation session.

If the recruiter starts to discuss your salary expectation range, here is a table with the recruiter response and suggested replies for you.

Recruiter says	Suggested reply
"Your range is higher than the budget for this role."	"I appreciate you letting me know. I am interested in the role, and salary is just one component. I'd like to learn more about the role, the team, and the organization and then revisit this."
"You're within the comp range for the role."	"Thanks for sharing that. Compensation is important to me, but so are the team and the organization. I'm excited to move forward."

As for which questions a candidate should ask, the recruiter is not going to have a lot of detail about the function of the role. Your time is limited, so it's best to focus your questions on the interview and hiring process. These questions should be:

- What is the ideal starting date for this role?
- What is the hiring process for this role?
- What can you tell me about the hiring manager?
- What traits helps people succeed in your organization?
- How many candidates are being interviewed, and how far along is the process?

These questions are critical to understand the organization's speed to hire and the process they follow. The last question might be a little provocative, especially the part about the number of candidates being interviewed. If that part of the question feels uncomfortable, then at least ask how far along they are in the process.

The question about the number of candidates and how far the process has moved along is great if you have time to ask it. Do you want to get feedback from the recruiter on the style and focus of the hiring manager? Do not expect a deep answer at this point but listen to how the recruiter describes them. Note what words they use about the manager's personality and work style. This is not definitive, but it gives you a baseline as you move ahead in the interview process.

A follow-up email to the recruiter is important, so make sure you have the recruiter's address before you get off the call. Keep your follow-up email short but include the following:

- your interest in the job and organization;
- how you are a good fit for the role—keep this to one to two sentences and provide examples;
- any scheduling challenges you might have—ideally you will tell them you're flexible, but if you have a tight schedule or other commitments that take up time in your day, let them know.

Finally, send them a LinkedIn connection request.

Inside the Recruiting Process

In larger organizations, you may well deal with multiple recruiters. The first recruiter is known as a "sourcer." Their job is to find qualified candidates, either through passive searches (most often using LinkedIn) or those who have submitted a résumé for a role.

The sourcer will hand off qualified candidates after the initial recruiter interview to a senior recruiter. That recruiter is in touch with the hiring manager and team. When a senior recruiter is involved, they will also do an interview that will be more like a hiring manager interview.

Potentially a third person might be involved: a scheduler. This is a recruiting team member or administrative staff member responsible for connecting candidates with hiring managers and interview teams. They have a tough job, as they are perpetually “herding cats.” Be nice to them! They will not have access to interview feedback; ask the senior recruiter for that info.

Also, the interview process may not happen in just three sections. This is particularly true for team interviews where getting everyone together during a single morning or afternoon can be daunting. Occasionally a team interview might take place over two sessions.

There are advantages and disadvantages to being in the hiring process either early or late. The advantage of being an early candidate is that you get to set the bar other candidates must meet. But the organization may want to interview everyone before making a final decision. This means you will wait longer for an answer.

Being a candidate later in the process has the opposite pluses and minuses of being an early candidate. The bar has likely been set, so you must meet or exceed the performance of the best candidate they have already interviewed. You will get an answer more quickly, however.

Hiring Manager Interviews

These interviews usually run sixty minutes and are the core of the interview process. Experienced hiring managers will have an agenda and will often share it up front.

Usually a hiring manager will focus most of the interview on the skills and experiences needed for the job. In other words, the interview will primarily focus on competency.

You will be asked some behavioral questions, but most of the interview will be based on skills and experience.

Hiring Manager Interview Logistics

Be ready to share "experience examples" describing how you've performed the required tasks spelled out in the job description. Typically, a job description lists three to five core tasks or functions. Be ready to explain how you have done each of these. The STAR model (situation, tactics, action, and results) is not necessary here; focus on the action and results.

Organize your answers into the steps you would follow. Most of the action steps will come from prior experience. But you can add in best practices or other processes you've seen others follow.

Expect follow-up questions. The hiring manager may want to "peel the onion" to get a deeper understanding of your steps, tools, and methods.

Research the hiring manager. Read the hiring manager's LinkedIn profile in detail. Note similarities you may share in education, prior jobs, or even shared contacts. See how they describe their career and work, again noting commonalities between you and them. See if you can find them on other social media sites as well.

A general rule of thumb about social media research: watch how you connect with hiring managers. LinkedIn is a safe connection before the interview, as is Twitter—but not Instagram or Facebook. Those cross the line into the hiring manager's personal life.

Read anything they have published or find out about conferences at which they've spoken. Your objective is to come into the interview with a well-rounded view of the hiring manager. During the interview, don't dump every bit of information you've uncovered about them but mention interesting facts and areas of alignment that might be specific to that part of the interview.

Ask the recruiter about the hiring manager's interview style and approach. Get an idea about what key areas the hiring manager will focus on, especially about job requirements. Remember, the recruiter is facilitating the process and can be an advocate for you. Don't hesitate to get pointers and ideas from them.

Questions to Prep For

"Tell me about yourself" may or may not come up; this will depend on the briefing the recruiter gave the hiring manager.

"What do you know about us?" This is where you bring out the research you've gathered in your targeting process.

Experience examples, as we mentioned above, are core to the interview.

Behavioral questions will come up. Hour-long interviews typically have one to two of these.

There usually isn't time to go into scenario questions, so these are not typically asked. But understand the process to answer them just in case you are.

Questions to Ask

Come in ready to ask questions, especially about where the team and projects are today—and where the hiring manager wants to take them in the future. You'll notice that one question we recommended when doing reach-outs also appears in this list:

- What are the key challenges and opportunities for your team this year (or the rest of year)?
- What are the key deliverables for this role in the first three months and six months?
- What knowledge or experience is essential to have for this role?
- What traits do you value most in a team member?
- How would you describe the rest of your team?

You may not have time for all five questions. Notice how we organize them. The first three are focused on execution. Asking at least two of these is important; it helps you gain more understanding of the role (which you can speak to) but also shows you are focused on delivering results.

If there is time, the last two questions are behavioral in nature but demonstrate your interest in being a solid member of the hiring manager's team.

Team Interviews

If you've made it this far, that's a good sign! You are one of a few candidates in the running, but the final interview process is also the most involved: the team interview. The organization wants you to meet with a cross section of the team and possibly one to two others from the organization at large.

Usually you will be meeting four to six people, either one-on-one or in small groups. It's less common to meet with an entire group at one time, though we'll describe one exception later in this section.

Don't discount team fit or cultural interviews. They are not light interviews; they are just as important. They will be more conversational, but that's the purpose: to see how you interact with others. We've often asked leaders from other teams to do "culture fit" interviews. Team fit interviewers have a strong voice in hiring decisions.

The objectives haven't changed: the organization still wants to validate the candidate's competence and culture fit. These interviews will be more targeted and will seek more detail in each category.

Notice how long each interview will be. Typically, they're under an hour. If one interview takes more than thirty minutes, it's likely they're planning a deep dive. Make sure you confirm this with the recruiter.

Obviously, there's a lot of scheduling to do, whether interviewing in person or virtually. It's not uncommon to see the scheduling coordinator move several people around or add and drop other people. As we said earlier, stay positive and upbeat as the schedule is locked down.

Team Interview Prep Work

Get a complete agenda, along with interviewer names, several days before the interview occurs. Do the same level of research you did for the hiring manager interview for each team interview member you meet.

As you do your research, keep in mind that some people who will interview you do not work on the team. They are likely internal customers of the team or are there to do a culture fit interview.

Ask the recruiter what topics each interviewer may cover with you. They may not be sure, but any information you can get to prepare will be helpful.

Prepare to give deeper experience answers. Experienced hiring managers and interviewing teams will set up an agenda that goes deeper into the key experience areas. The hiring manager will ask team members to validate what they heard but will also drill deeper in case the manager has perceived gaps.

Think back through the hiring manager interview, and expect to go into more detail describing the steps you took and decisions you made along the way.

Try and match the schedule to your personal "peak time." Are you a morning person or an afternoon person? If possible, try to schedule the team interview during your personal peak time, when your energy is the strongest. A key objective is to have the best possible energy for as long as possible.

It's a small thing, but if they are not indicated, ask about breaks. Sometimes in a rush to build a schedule, the organization may forget to give you a chance to pause. That's almost always accidental, so be sure to ask about breaks if you don't see them in the schedule.

Questions to Prep For

Brand statement—At least one person will ask you about this, likely a culture fit interviewer.

Experience answers—As we already mentioned, these will likely come from a team member who understands the functions in more detail. They will want to hear more detail about your methods and approaches to the key job responsibilities. They are following up on the hiring manager's questions to revalidate but also to get more insight.

This is a great opportunity for you to understand more about the team and their operations. Don't simply provide answers—ask questions back. Learn about their operations and methods and see where you align and differ. We've often seen these conversations become a great information exchange, along with cementing your culture fit on the team.

Behavioral questions—Be prepared for all five of the questions outlined earlier in this chapter. Several if not all of them will come up in one form or another. Be conversational, not rigid. Don't tell the whole story with all the details all at once. Let the interviewers ask questions to further understand.

Case-study and real-world scenarios—During team interviews is when real-world scenarios will be asked. Understand the process we shared earlier and think about the information discussed during the hiring manager interview. If they ask for a case-study or real-world scenario, it will probably be about one of the areas you've already discussed.

Questions to Ask

The questions you need to ask fall into two groups of recipients: the team interviewers and the culture fit interviewers. Remember that these interviews will also typically be thirty to forty-five minutes long, so you may only have a chance to ask one or two questions.

Here are a few team or functional interviewer questions:

- What are the key challenges and opportunities for your team this year (or the rest of year)?
- What knowledge or experience is essential to have for this role?

- What tools and resources are essential to know to be a strong team member?
- What new initiatives are coming, and how are you preparing for them?
- What steps would you take, if you were me, to ramp up and quickly help the team?

Here are some culture team fit interviewer questions:

- How would you describe the culture?
- What are the key challenges and opportunities the organization has this year (or the rest of year)?
- What traits make someone successful in this organization?
- How have you grown since you've been here?
- What things do you like most about working here?

Following Up

Since more people are involved, you'll have more following up to do. Ideally you'll have email addresses for each interviewer, though that's not always the case. If you have their email addresses, then send them a short email that follows the hiring manager email outline:

- a sincere (but not over-the-top) thank-you for their time; mention something they shared;
- your key takeaways about the role of the team and the company; keep this short: just a couple of sentences;

- your continued interest in the role;
- any information you want to emphasize or might not have gotten a chance to share; shorter is better.

Send a LinkedIn invite as well with another thank-you for their time. Don't be disappointed if they don't accept; some interviewers don't feel comfortable with this, but they often appreciate the effort.

Send the hiring manager another note, this time thanking them for the chance to meet the team members. Include one or two insights you gained about the role and the team. Finally, clearly state your continued interest in working for them. As always, keep this short.

Finally, the recruiter gets an email that's like the hiring manager note. The only addition is the status on the rest of your job search, especially if you have other interviews or are close to receiving another offer. Don't overplay this, but keeping the recruiter in the loop is important.

Interview Question Preparation

As you saw in the interview logistics, there are various categories of questions to consider. By working through *The Job Search Manifesto*, you will be prepared to answer two key questions: "Tell me about yourself" and "What do you know about us?"

Tell me about yourself will be answered with your brand statement, slightly tailored to the role and the organization. We emphasized in the chapter on brand statements the importance of articulating your skills and accomplishments. In an interview, you share them but add in how they apply to the role and the organization you're interviewing for.

EXERCISE: WRITE THE "TELL ME ABOUT YOURSELF" ANSWER

Take your core brand statement and apply it to the specific role and organization. Write this down; it should be pretty straightforward. Remember you will be delivering this verbally, so say it out loud. You want it to sound conversational.

What do you know about us? This is an easy place to score points. Take what you've learned about the organization: its key challenges and initiatives. Then describe how you see the role and how it can contribute to moving the organization ahead. Don't worry if you're not 100 percent accurate; that's not the point. Showing that you did solid research and synthesized it is key.

EXERCISE: WRITE THE "WHAT DO YOU KNOW ABOUT US?" ANSWER

Provide one or to two-sentence overview in your own words. Then discuss the organization's current state and aspirations, also in one to two sentences. Tie them together by sharing how you see the role helping the organization move forward.

Again, remember that you will be saying this, so practice saying it out loud to keep the tone conversational.

Control the Interview Flow by Checking In

You have compelling, high-impact stories to share, and you want to put them all out there. It's natural to want to tell every detail for each of your interview stories. This is often triggered by concern that you've left an important detail out of the story—and that detail might be the key reason they would hire you. But this tell-all strategy is self-defeating.

The tell-all approach can confuse an interviewer by potentially overloading them information. Getting inundated with all the details and facts of the story might actually cause the interviewer to *miss* relevant information.

A way to control this is through the simple check-in method. Here's how it works: after you tell a story, or provide a long, detailed answer, stop yourself and ask the interviewer one of these questions (or develop your own):

- "Was this what you were looking for?"
- "Did this help?"
- "Any questions come to mind?"

The check-in method is what often happens when someone is doing a presentation with a slide deck. Before they press the next slide button, the presenter will often ask, "Are there any questions?" It's the same idea, just applied in an interview.

Here's what checking in does for both the candidate and the interviewer.

The interviewer is given a chance to process the story and then dive into areas they want to learn more about. They can go in the direction that matches their interests and needs instead of being given every detail.

The candidate gets a chance to pause and take a break for a moment. Instead of being perpetually "on" during the whole interview, this can create a moment to gather their thoughts. A check-in takes the pressure off.

A final benefit to checking in is that it can trigger a more conversational interview. When the candidate invites feedback and questions, it's an opening to move to an information exchange, instead of the "I ask, you reply" interview format.

Behavioral Interview Questions

Behavioral interviews are a useful method (when done well) to understand the two areas of candidate evaluation: competence and culture fit. Keep that in mind as you read this chapter and prep for future interviews. Interviewing is meant to evaluate just these two areas: a candidate's competence (ability to perform the tasks of the job) and culture fit (the ability to team up well and be a positive member of the team and organization).

The other interview phobia we have often encountered in our coaching is about having the perfect answer. Too frequently we see candidates lock up or really stumble when they're given a scenario and they cannot produce a complete detailed solution. What they're missing is the real reason recruiters ask scenario-based questions: we want to understand the process a candidate follows, not necessarily the completed answer.

We've broken this chapter into segments hacking behavioral questions and learning to give process-based answers. We also offer a couple of tools and approaches to make the interview more conversational—and to take some pressure off candidates.

Behavioral interview questions are questions in several topic areas that require the candidate to share a story on that topic. We believe that there are four topic categories; if you prep for them, you should be well prepared for an interview. The categories are:

- most significant achievement
- lessons learned—the "failure question"
- "tell me about a time" questions
- we focus on just three areas:
  - conflict
  - ambiguity
  - scaling, growth, and capacity
- real-world or case-study questions

Having well-structured stories for each of these four categories will put you in a solid place for interviews. Below are structures and examples for each.

"Most Significant Achievement" Question

Right up front we want to stress that this question is not intended to get you to brag; it's a method to learn the process you followed to deliver a significant achievement or outcome. We see people get uncomfortable thinking they must lavish themselves with self-praise in their answer. That is not the case.

Lou Adler, a recruiting industry leader says has these thoughts about the Most Significant Achievement Question in his book *Hire with Your Head*:

> It's pretty remarkable when you think about what an interviewer could earn about a candidate just by asking

> about his or her biggest accomplishment. It would include things like talent, motivation, critical thinking, personality, character, values, team or individual focus, self-awareness, communication skills, overall ability, cultural fit and commitment to name a few. (16)

In prepping for a most significant achievement (or MSA) answer, these are a couple of keys.

First, your MSA does not have to be from your latest role. Do not get caught up about using something you did well in your last job as your MSA unless it really is. Your MSA should be something you are genuinely proud of and that had strong impact. That pride needs to come through. We've heard MSA stories that came from people's college years, early career, and even from volunteering. The power of the story comes from your pride in it.

Second, apply as much of the MSA story as you can to the role for which you are interviewing. Tying the MSA story to the role for which you are interviewing is important, but don't try to stretch it too far. Like the story itself, you want this to be genuine. Some areas where you can tie your MSA to the current role include acting while learning, delivering the solution under a tight deadline, and getting buy-in and help from multiple groups.

Third, if it feels uncomfortable and too much like bragging, then emphasize that the group achieved this.

If it still feels like bragging or too self-centered, try emphasizing the team around you. Instead of saying, "I brought the solution in early and ten percent below budget," you could say, "The team I led brought the solution in early and ten percent below budget." It's a subtle change, but some people find it more comfortable that way.

Just remember that when you focus on the team, you will have to clearly explain your role and major tasks. If you assembled the team, say that.

Here's a sample MSA story:

> Sales and engineering leaders were always in conflict about what the sales team was offering as features for our enterprise solution. This was a constant source of friction between the groups. I was asked by leadership to build a new pre-sales solution architect team that would work closely with the sales team at every point of the sales process.
>
> It was a heavy customer-facing role to help understand the customer issues and needs, then provide as many standard solutions as possible. When a true custom need was identified, the solution architect team would provide detailed specifications back to engineering. We would also keep the customer continually informed about the cost and time to deliver the custom solutions.
>
> Within six months, sales grew 30 percent, and custom engineering work shrunk by over 50 percent. We were delivering more products in less time and utilizing our engineering resources much better.
>
> I've used the communication skills I gained from this role again and again in my career. I believe the role we're

discussing here requires the ability to talk with a large range of stakeholders and really understand their needs and positions.

In the sample story, you see the STAR (situation, tension, action, and result) model we described and used in the chapter on LinkedIn. Here we add another element: tie-back. How does your MSA story tie back to the needs of the role for which you are interviewing? We use another model for this story, START, for situation, tension, action, result, and tie-back.

EXERCISE: BUILD THE FRAMEWORK FOR YOUR "MOST SIGNIFICANT ACHIEVEMENT" ANSWER

Write the bullet points for your MSA story using the START framework.

Situation	
Tension	
Action	
Result	
Tie-back	

EXERCISE: WRITE THE NARRATIVE FOR YOUR "MOST SIGNIFICANT ACHIEVEMENT" ANSWER

Take the bullet points and put them into a written narrative—think of it as a script. You want to be able to tell this story in about sixty to ninety-seconds, which is longer than it seems.

"Lessons Learned" Questions

First, be honest and own your mistakes, but don't be a martyr. Own up to your errors and your team's but be matter of fact. No drama is needed.

Second, don't throw anyone under the bus. Blaming others for the problems is a red flag to an interviewer—don't do it. Even if the error was caused by others, blaming them shows a lack of empathy or emotional intelligence. It raises serious questions about your teamwork and culture fit.

Third, explain how you learned to prevent this error from happening again. This is the most important part of the answer. Providing details about your learning and how you made corrections is the key expectation from a failure story. As recruiters, we would also ask that question because we wanted our organization to learn from the mistakes a candidate had already seen and fixed. Organizations can benefit from the knowledge gained from a candidate's failure situation and ideally avoid the same mistake. That's the positive result from a failure story.

Here's a sample "lessons learned" story:

> I joined a medical center as the medical information director four months before they were to be audited by a national organization for certification. The audit was a critical event, and the medical center had barely passed the last time. I had led a successful audit at my prior job less than a year earlier, so I was confident I could successfully lead them through this.
>
> After I joined and started doing mock audits, I found the facility was far behind in its preparation. The processes and methods they used to document and audit care were inadequate and pointed to a lot of need for training for many groups in the medical center, especially the doctors.
>
> I had a lot of dialogues with the medical staff and leadership team and took immediate steps—all standard operating procedures—but got strong and immediate pushback. Doctors were upset that I was "threatening them," and several complained loudly. After talking with the leadership team, we modified our approach and became more unified in our message. I dialed back my approach and became more diplomatic than I had been.

We got through the audit and were again certified, but I learned that my approach had to change. What worked for one medical center didn't translate to the other. My key lesson was to listen and learn first before I act. And to be more flexible and quickly iterate my approaches when needed.

In the role you're considering me for, listening and being flexible and iterative with action steps are important. I learned that lesson and have applied it successfully throughout my career.

EXERCISE: BUILD THE FRAMEWORK FOR YOUR "LESSONS LEARNED" ANSWER

Write the bullet points for your "lesson learned" story using the START framework. The results row should include the lessons or takeaways you gained from the experience.

Situation	
Tension	
Action	
Result	

Tie-back	

EXERCISE: WRITE THE NARRATIVE FOR YOUR "LESSONS LEARNED" ANSWER

Take the bullet points and put them into a written narrative; think of it as a script. You want to be able to tell this story in about sixty to ninety-seconds, which is longer than it seems.

"Tell Me about a Time" (TMAAT) Questions

"Tell me about a time" questions are behavioral questions in which people ask for specific examples where you dealt with the question's topic; you answer by providing a sample story. TMAAT questions are almost always a part of interviews.

People ask a ton of sample questions, and we've seen candidates spend hours and hours prepping for them. With our mission to make job searching and interviewing a more straightforward process, we've done a lot of analysis and testing of these questions to simplify the prep work and to make candidates able to provide more meaningful answers. Below is our model to simplify these types of questions.

TMAAT questions come in a huge range, but they tend to focus on just three categories: (1) conflict; (2) ambiguity; and (3) scaling, growth, or capacity.

Those who ask conflict questions seek examples of when you dealt with debate, conflict, or disagreement. The person asking the question is looking for how you handled the conflict and what the outcome was.

When people ask ambiguity questions, they want to learn how you dealt with projects or roles that had a lot of questions or not a lot of guidance or direction. With these questions, they're seeking to learn how you created clarity and moved the project forward.

People who ask scaling, growth, or capacity questions are looking for situations you resolved when asked to grow a project or team faster than expected. The questions here also can involve dealing with capacity issues. For example, you or your team are already working overtime, and another time-intense project shows up. How do you prioritize and balance the workload?

There are universal elements that apply to all TMAAT questions, no matter the category. They are as follows.

One common question is "Explain the process you followed to address or resolve the issue." As interviewers, we are not looking for perfect endings; that's not the point of these questions. We want to understand the process a candidate followed to deal with the problem. If you can clearly explain your process, then it shows maturity and emotional intelligence. These situations will happen again; your story demonstrates that you have a plan to address them.

Another benefit to understanding the candidate's process is that interviewers can evaluate how your method would work or *not* work in their culture. That does not mean a candidate is disqualified; it just triggers astute interviewers to share more information about the structure and culture of the organization.

A second common question is "Explain in detail how you communicated." At their core, TMAAT questions show how candidates communicate, especially when under stress. Stressing how you communicate throughout the process with all parties involved is critical. Usually two or more parties are involved:

- the person or group that is the focus of the TMAAT question;
- managers and leaders the interviewer reports to and who need detailed status reports;
- other stakeholders with an interest in the outcome

How you communicate isn't just how you communicate at the beginning or the end of the process but also during. Often, we hear candidates leave out how they communicate updates. It's important to explain all three.

For all TMAAT questions, you want to explain both your process and how you communicated. The model we use to build TMAAT stories includes "situation," which generally consists of who is involved, process, and result.

Situation is a brief summation of the candidate's story and how it matches up with the TMAAT question. As we emphasized in the section on early interview prep, you want to make sure the story is a good match.

Candidates need to be clear about *who is involved*. Typically, there are two or more groups. In a TMAAT conflict story with a customer, one party is obviously the customer. The other party would be management and leadership. Communicating with them throughout the situation is a key part of the process and needs to be included in the story. Include all the parties involved and how you communicated with them at each stage: initially, updates, and during the conclusion.

Process is the heart of the story, and it is easy to get deep into details. Going into details here can cause the story to become confusing and the interviewer to lose track of the core messages.

Be brief when you discuss the *result*; you should not try to dive deeply here either. Also, be realistic with the outcome. Remember that the interviewer wants to understand your process and how you communicate in these situations. A positive result is great, but not all situations end with a 100 percent resolution. The candidate needs to balance optimism and realism. Don't oversell the story.

In the next section, we'll go into each of the three TMAAT scenarios.

TMAAT Conflict Questions

Here are some sample TMAAT conflict questions:

- "Tell me about a time when you dealt with an unhappy customer."

- "How have you dealt with situations where your boss didn't understand an important issue about a project and was being stubborn?"

- "Tell me about a time when you had honest disagreements with a peer about a plan of action."

Think about which group you would deal with the most in the role and ideally provide a conflict story that involved that group, remembering that there are only four groups you deal with: (1) managers or leaders, (2) peers, (3) staff or reports, and (4) customers.

Conflict stories really center around communication more than any other question. Focus on the steps you took or the process you followed in dealing with the situation.

EXERCISE : BUILD THE FRAMEWORK FOR YOUR TMAAT CONFLICT STORY

Write the bullet points for your TMAAT conflict story using the START framework. The results row should include the lessons or takeaways you gained from the experience.

Situation	
Tension	
Action	
Result	
Tie-back	

EXERCISE: WRITE THE NARRATIVE FOR TMAAT CONFLICT QUESTIONS

Take the bullet points and put them into a written narrative; think of it as a script. You want to be able to tell this story in about sixty to ninety-seconds, which is longer than it seems.

TMAAT Ambiguity Questions

Here are some sample TMAAT ambiguity questions:

- "Tell me about a time when you were asked to work on a time-sensitive project with little guidance or structure."
- "What have you done when a customer asks for assistance but was vague about what they needed and expected?"
- "What have you done when someone who reports to you is struggling with a project but can't explain the problem or what kind of help they need?"

With ambiguity stories, the core objective is to understand how a candidate reached clarity during an ambiguous situation. Typically, that involves multiple steps of questioning, evaluating, and reaching a series of smaller agreements.

EXERCISE: BUILD THE FRAMEWORK FOR TMAAT AMBIGUITY STORY

Write the bullet points for your TMAAT ambiguity story using the START framework. The results row should include the lessons or takeaways you gained from the experience.

Situation	
Tension	
Action	
Result	
Tie-back	

EXERCISE: WRITE THE NARRATIVE FOR TMAAT AMBIGUITY STORY

Take the bullet points and put them into a written narrative; think of it as a script. You want to be able to tell this story in about sixty to ninety-seconds, which is longer than it seems.

TMAAT Scaling, Growth, and Capacity Questions

Here are some sample TMAAT scaling, growth, and capacity questions:

- "Tell me about a time when you and your team were already buried in work and another high-priority project was handed to you."

- "What have you done when forecasts and models say that your customer base will grow rapidly, faster than the current headcount can support?"
- "Tell me about a time when your team came up with a great idea to improve a product, but implementing it would have either delayed completion or eliminated other new features in order to meet the delivery date."

EXERCISE: BUILD THE FRAMEWORK FOR TMAAT SCALING, GROWTH, AND CAPACITY STORY

Write the bullet points for your TMAAT scaling, growth, and capacity story using the START framework. The results row should include the lessons or takeaways you gained from the experience.

Situation	
Tension	
Action	
Result	
Tie-back	

EXERCISE: WRITE THE NARRATIVE FOR TMAAT SCALING, GROWTH, AND CAPACITY STORY

Take the bullet points and put them into a written narrative; think of it as a script. You want to be able to tell this story in about sixty to ninety-seconds, which is longer than it seems.

Case Studies and Real-World Scenarios

The last interview question category to prepare for is case-study or scenario questions. These are usually real-world challenges the organization is facing and the person they hire will be facing. Much like with TMAAT questions, the candidate may not have a fully formed answer with a true resolution. And this is where we often see candidates lock up.

Some candidates feel they must have experienced and solved *all* elements of the problem. They feel that without a complete story, they can't give an adequate answer. As a result, their answer and their demeanor come across as tentative and nervous. This is sad, because as interviewers we are *not* looking for a completely baked answer.

Much like a TMAAT question, interviewers are looking for the *process* the candidate followed to address the case-study question. This means that a candidate needs to clearly share the steps they would follow to address the issue in the scenario.

Here are some sample case-study or real-world scenario questions:

- "If you join us, we'd want you to lead an upgrade to our accounting system; we've outgrown the current application. Our concern is our current data is incomplete, and the upgrade project seems to be getting more complex as we go along. How would you approach this?"

- "Our customer satisfaction scores are falling, especially in the last year. We're frustrated because we've put a lot of effort into training our support teams and improving our systems. What would you do to reverse this trend?"

- "We're always delayed in our go-to-market execution, both for new products and product upgrades. Where have you dealt with this, and what would you do to help us stop the delays?"

Since the range of scenarios is specific to job roles, this section is a thought process rather than one of building out the story. We want to focus more on the "assembly process" or prep work needed to answer these questions.

The best way to organize these answers is to "chunk" or break down the path you would follow into steps. As we described earlier, some of the action steps will come from prior experience. But it's not unusual to not have done every process step and to rely on best practices or other processes you've seen other people perform.

Remember: the key here is to assemble the action plan, not to have done it, and not to have direct experience in each step. Don't get hung up on that.

EXERCISE: BUILD THE CONTENT TO ANSWER A PROCESS QUESTION

Choose a process question you expect to answer and write out the steps you would follow. Also check whether the step you're documenting is something you have done (your experience) or is based on best practices.

Process step	Description	Experience or best practice
Step 1		☐ Experience ☐ Best practice
Step 2		☐ Experience ☐ Best practice
Step 3		☐ Experience ☐ Best practice
Step 4		☐ Experience ☐ Best practice

We've also provided the START answer format for reference. As you answer a scenario or real-world question, you deliver the key information in the action part of your answer.

Situation	
Tension	
Action	
Result	
Tie-back	

Following Up and Sample Work

After the hiring manager interview, you're going to follow up with both the senior recruiter and the hiring manager. Here are steps for a recommended follow-up email with the recruiter:

- Thank them for setting up the interview.
- Share the key areas of the interview; keep this to one or two sentences.

- Emphasize your continued interest in the role.
- Update the recruiter on scheduling and any other relevant information about your job search; this is not to play a game but to keep the recruiter well informed.

The hiring manager follow-up email should include the following:

- sincere (but not over-the-top) thank-you for their time, and a mention of something they shared
- the key takeaways you had about the role of the team and the company; keep this short (just a couple of sentences);
- your continued interest in the role;
- information you want to emphasize or might not have gotten a chance to share; shorter is better.

For some interviews, there might be a project or sample work to do. For engineering interviews this is quite common, especially in software engineering. But we've seen them come up sometimes in sales, operations, and marketing.

The purpose of these projects is to demonstrate competence. It is not to steal ideas or methods, which is why reputable organizations keep their projects tightly focused. Think of them as case-study projects.

These projects typically take between two to four hours. If you're finding your time going beyond this, check in with the recruiter and give them a status report. Most organizations do not want candidates putting that much time into the project.

There are two other elements to keep in mind about team interviews: the role of the recruiter and hiring manager and group presentations.

It's common for the recruiter to be on the agenda for a team interview. Typically, we'd greet the candidate and spend about fifteen minutes before the main interview began. We'd often peek our heads in during the interview to check on things, especially during breaks. Finally, we would do a debrief at the end of the interview process.

As a candidate, use the recruiter debrief time effectively. Reiterate next steps and share your observations and strong interest in the role. This is a time to reconfirm the basics of the job, including salary, start date, and the time line to making the hiring decision. You can also ask if the recruiter has any feedback, but they often won't share much. They've probably only heard snippets of feedback from just a few interviewers.

Hiring managers will also play a role in team interviews. They may want to do a follow-up interview to gain more clarity and might take a full interview slot to do this. Other hiring managers might do a short introduction at the beginning of the team interviews or a recap at the end.

As for group presentations, earlier in the chapter we talked about some organizations asking for a small project to be completed prior to the team interview. That case study or project will likely be discussed multiple times during the team interview. In rare cases, a candidate might be asked to do a group presentation. Don't panic as you read this; it usually only happens during engineering or technical interviews or sales interviews.

These group presentations are almost always planned ahead of time and are usually just a summary of the project you've worked on. If you're asked to do a presentation like this, you can use the smart format Azure presentation template. Typically, these presentations take less than an hour and are conversational. Interview teams want to see your group communication skills along with your ability to answer questions on the fly.

In engineering presentations, they are looking to understand your thought process and the tools and methods you use to reach your conclusions.

In all cases, be prepared to answer questions but to also ask clarifying questions if their question isn't clear.

These presentations can be stressful, but if you've done all the prep work we recommend here, the presentation should not be daunting, except for the butterflies that inevitably sometimes show up

Summary

Interviewing can be much less stressful when you have a plan; the goal of this chapter was to create one. We include detailed models you can use to build out your stories and set the right tone.

- Remember your brand statement. A longer version of it answers the question, "Tell me about yourself."

- Understand the logistics of the interview process, which usually include a recruiter interview, hiring manager interview, and team interview. Each is different, and we've shown you how to prepare for them.

- For behavioral interviews, be ready with stories for these five questions: (1) most significant achievement; (2) lessons learned; three "tell me about a time" stories, including (3) conflict, (4) ambiguity, and (5) growth/scaling and prioritization.

- Check in. Never tell a story without validating that the interviewer has understood it.

- Ask strong questions to pull out and understand the key challenges the organization is facing.

- Prep for problem-solving and case studies by clearly explaining the process you would follow.

- Know how to discuss compensation with the recruiter.

JOB OFFERS AND NEGOTIATIONS

Manifesto

- The key to maximizing a job offer is to understand all the components of the offer.
- Know what is easy to negotiate—and what is hard or can't be negotiated.
- The offer negotiation process should be a collaboration, not a contentious disagreement.
- You set the tone for your relationship with the organization as you negotiate—and so do they.

Catherine: Her Knowledge Was Golden

Catherine was making a significant change, moving from a scientific product to a social media tech company. Her experience was both in marketing and operations; she worked closely with her career coach to demonstrate how her experience and accomplishments were completely transferable.

After interviewing with three major tech companies, Catherine was caught in a pleasant dilemma: one company had offered her a role, while another was ready to schedule her final on-site interview. The asynchronous timing made the negotiation process a little tricky, but having done a lot of research and preplanning, she was able to gracefully maneuver through the process.

The key to Catherine's negotiation success was a healthy understanding of each company's interview process and how their offers would be structured. She had strong existing relationships in both organizations who provided her with key information that included salary and compensation data.

Her first-choice company was also the first to extend an offer. The three major components of the offer were base salary, annual bonus, and stock grants or RSUs (restricted stock units). Working with her coach on the negotiation, they built a detailed reply for each element. The initial offer was a bit low, but not by a huge amount.

Catherine knew that the company often gave sign-on bonuses; the base salary was about 15 percent lower than comparable roles in the company, and she knew that the stock grant or RSU could be raised. So she and her coach strategized increases in all these areas.

Before Catherine reached back out to the recruiter, she had a coaching session focused on establishing the tone she would set for the negotiation. They agreed she'd tell the recruiter that she wanted to "collaborate with him to make this happen."

When Catherine reconnected with the recruiter, he was pleased to hear she wanted to accept the offer. Once she had established legitimate enthusiasm for the opportunity, it was time to share her counterproposal. The recruiter listened to her offers on salary and RSUs, along with the request for a sign-on bonus. He promised to share her proposal internally and get back to her with feedback—and potentially the company's counter.

In less than half a day, the recruiter came back with a counter. The company had increased the salary by 5 percent and 10 percent more in stock grants. They also added a small sign-on bonus. Catherine thanked him but added additional information to her request.

She explained that her counter was based on the other company's typical offer for her experience level and role. She was clear that she didn't have an offer yet but was setting up an on-site final interview. If the recruiter could get the numbers closer to hers, she would accept the offer and not do the final interview with the other company.

In less than two hours, the recruiter called back with a third offer that met Catherine's RSU request and added more to her base salary. The surprise was the sign-on bonus. It jumped 20 percent.

The recruiter told her they really wanted her, and this was their way to show their seriousness. Catherine happily signed the offer, notified the other company, and started her new job with a hefty raise in her total compensation.

About This Chapter

We've seen a lot of issues come up during salary negotiations, but they often aren't about the offer—they're about the candidate. Issues usually arise about salary inequity, company values, imposter syndrome, and personal and family transitions. Negotiations often bring up negative feelings about self-worth and self-esteem, especially when compounded with money and job titles.

The flip side is that compensation partnering can be a positive experience, especially if you take steps to set your expectations early. Your goals in negotiating a job offer should of course be to come away with better compensation but also more opportunities to learn and grow within an organization you believe in.

Focus on four action steps for job offer negotiations:

- stay grounded to your values;
- collaborate, by managing your tone and presence;
- become knowledgeable about industry and career function, market compensation, company leveling, and the role; then be prepared to showcase that knowledge;
- offer details.

We'll explore each of these items with a deep focus on the strategy associated with each component of an offer.

Stay Grounded to Your Values

At the beginning of the book, we had you identify and build out your values and next-job attributes. Your list helped refine your targeting and interviewing strategy; now those same values are also critical components of your offer negotiation.

When you consider the values and attributes you seek in an opportunity, how do the company and role stack up? How much of what you're seeking is in alignment with this job? If you think you've found 100 percent of your objectives, we are officially nervous, because *there is no perfect job.*

Whenever we've heard that a job (or a candidate, for that matter) is "perfect," something is usually wrong. The candidate is settling for a job for which they are overqualified (and might get bored with quickly), or the job has problems or challenges that have been masked during the interview.

Dawn Graham said it well in her book *Switchers: How Smart Professionals Change Careers—and Seize Success*, in which she described the trade-off between salary and work-life balance:

> Consider the big picture. Salary is a key motivator, but other aspects of a job contribute to overall satisfaction. If your new job energizes you, reduces stress, or allows you to spend more time on hobbies that give you pleasure, perhaps the trade-off in pay is worth it. (9)

Focus on Collaboration

We have worked on over seven hundred offers, both as recruiters and coaches. As an internal recruiting leader, Mike has negotiated offers on behalf of dozens of companies. One of the areas we feel strongly about is the negotiating tone you set and the style you should follow.

Too often we've seen people approach negotiation from one of two extremes: being overly aggressive or feeling powerless. Neither one should be the case. During the interview process, you demonstrated that you could help the organization solve their existing challenges, and you're a good team and culture fit. Those two facts give you power.

In Catherine's story, she made sure the recruiter knew she wanted the job and wanted to collaborate to make it happen. Her approach considered the recruiter's perspective on negotiation. Here's an example of typical recruiter language to a candidate:

> The team was impressed with you and your background. We've all seen the value you'd bring, and I'm excited to share

> this offer and have you join us. I'll give you all the numbers in a moment, but I also want to set a tone. I believe in making this a conversation, not a hard-core negotiation. My goal is for you to be excited to join us, and the offer adds to that.

Studies on successful job offer negotiations have identified the five types of negotiating strategies outlined below, with varying levels of success.

Collaborating	Both sides engaging in problem-solving to reach the best possible outcome for both sides
Competing	Focusing on maximizing your own outcomes with little concern for those of others
Accommodating	Putting the other party's concerns first
Compromising	Trying to reach a middle ground
Avoiding	Dodging negotiations altogether

As noted in a Harvard Law School blog post discussing previous research, two styles were most successful for a candidate in one study, but only one left the negotiators more satisfied:

> Those who chose to negotiate salary, rather than accepting the offer on the table, increased their starting pay by an average of $5,000, primarily by using competing and collaborating strategies. Those who behaved competitively did better than those who focused on collaboration, but collaborators were more satisfied than competitive bargainers with the negotiation process. By contrast,

> compromising and accommodating strategies were not linked to salary gains. (12)

The collaborative approach has other benefits. First, you are encouraging the recruiter to become your advocate. The recruiter is mediating the offer between a candidate and the company's leadership. As the candidate, you want a collaborator helping to advocate your adjustments to the offer.

The second benefit is building your internal reputation *before* you join. We've seen many examples where a candidate was competitive during negotiations and pushed hard for their counteroffer. They didn't consider that the leadership team was tracking the process. Mike had C-level executives who approved a tough negotiation's final offer, then say the candidate had "better be able to walk on water" or that "the candidate has a target on their back."

We are not advocating you be passive—in fact, quite the opposite. Having solid data, knowing your values, and offering to work with the recruiter is a position of strength. But keep in mind that the tone you set during negotiations can create a positive or negative bias before you even start.

Author and organizational psychologist Adam Grant describes the approach and attitude this way:

> In a comprehensive analysis of 28 studies, the most successful negotiators cared as much about the other party's success as their own. They refused to see negotiations as win-lose or the world as zero-sum. They understood that before you could claim value, you needed to create value. They didn't declare victory until they could help everyone win. (13)

Setting a tone of collaboration can make a big difference. Catherine found that the recruiter went from being helpful to becoming a full-on advocate for her hire. Setting this tone early is also important as you join the organization, especially if the organization is small.

Become Knowledgeable and Be Ready to Share It

The adage "knowledge is power" is a good starting point but needs some adjustment when applied to job offer negotiation. We recommend that acquiring the *right* knowledge and sharing it at the *right* time is power.

Knowledge you need to collect includes the following:

- the components of the organization's offer early in the hiring process
- the organization's salary range for the position—again, early in the hiring process
- current information on the marketplace, from multiple sources, including compensation sites (we'll list several sites)
- your self-ranking of the importance of each offer component
- your schedule to start
- how the job aligns with your career short term and your long-term values and aspirations.

The first five bullets are mostly facts with some extrapolation thrown in. We'll be walking through how to organize the first five. But the sixth bullet, on the alignment of the job to your values and aspirations, is important—and will take us full circle.

Offer Details

When you receive an offer, it's typically broken into two parts: compensation and benefits. Usually, people spend their time looking at the compensation salary offer, but understanding benefits is also important. Your negotiation plan needs to start with understanding all the components or "levers" of an offer.

We use the analogy of levers in job offer negotiations to consider each major offer element as something you can adjust easily or, in some cases, not adjust at all. There can also be a relationship between levers: if one goes up, another might go down.

Let's explore lever or offer components. We'll indicate which components are easily negotiable—and others that are less so.

The core of an offer is the compensation side, but we're adding a common challenge to the mix. Let's look at these key elements: salary, bonus, commission, relocation, start date, and job title. Here's the baseline of knowledge you want for each.

Salary. Besides the amount, you need to know how often you are paid (monthly, bimonthly, or every other week) and what days are paydays. It's also helpful to know the review cycles. This can be useful information during the negotiation. If the salary isn't in the expected range, and they aren't budging, consider asking for an early or "out-of-cycle" review.

Bonus. Does the company have a bonus program? If so, is it based on individual, team, or company performance, or a mix? What is the amount or percentage of the bonus, and what is the payout cycle—annual, quarterly, or other? Finally, what is the historical payout—how often have people been paid out the total amount or more?

Commission. This is typically found in sales roles, but sometimes sales support staff receive commissions. If you're in a sales role, make sure you get a solid understanding of the structure and compensation of the commission program. Usually a company has a commission plan they provide; make sure to request it.

Pay attention to how the commission structure works. Is everything you sell commissionable, and are there different commission levels for different products or services? Find out how well the sales team is doing—are they hitting their numbers, and what is the average commission payout? Get clear on the frequency of commission payouts: monthly, quarterly, semiannually, or annually.

One important thing to understand is "ramp." Some companies with complex products or long sales cycles will provide a commission ramp for a few months when you start. Learn about how long the ramp lasts (usually a few months) and the amount.

RSUs or stock options. If a company is offering stock or equity, understanding it is key. Restricted stock units apply when a company's stock is publicly traded. You are given a dollar amount, typically at or under the current stock price.

For stock options, these are typically provided while a company is still private. You are given an amount of stock that has a value that is defined by the company's board of directors. There is no immediate cash value for these shares, only the hope that the company will be acquired or go public, which makes the shares tangible and valuable.

In both cases you vest or take ownership of these over a period. A typical vesting cycle is over four years. You vest or take ownership of 25 percent of the shares on your first-year anniversary. You then vest incrementally (monthly or quarterly, for example) the remaining three years.

Though four years is a typical vesting cycle, we've seen varied vesting cycles. Understanding the RSU and stock option program is key for a better position in relation to cash compensation.

Relocation expenses *(if applicable)*. If you must relocate to take the job, make sure you discuss relocation expenses. Often companies will have a set relocation amount, but that number can vary depending on the seniority of the role, the distance to relocate, and any spouse/partner or family member relocations.

Typically, relocation is paid in two ways: either an up-front payout, like a sign-on bonus, or through reimbursed expenses, which requires you to submit an expense report. Get a good understanding of how the payout works.

Larger organizations may use relocation services or even have them in-house. As you get into negotiations, you may want to speak to someone from the service to understand how they can assist. Only ask about this if you are relocating.

Start date. Start dates are often thought of later in the process but can often cause last-minute hang-ups. We will talk about paid time off (PTO) policies in the next section, but if you have a significant trip scheduled that might affect your start date, you should bring it up before you get the offer.

The reason is that the team might be excited to get you started, only to find out it might be delayed by a few extra weeks. We've seen negotiations grind to a halt, as this issue may require new approvals from senior management.

A strong suggestion is that if you are looking to take an extended break (more than four weeks) before you can start a new job, you need to think about your job search timing. We have shut down candidates when we found out they couldn't start for three more months. Make sure you can commit to a start date that fits your life but also doesn't negatively affect your new team.

Exceptions do exist, of course. If you're a new grad and have accepted the position before you graduate, you'll likely start after graduation. Weddings or other major life events are also understood. Don't hold this information for the last minute.

We've always been surprised how often people don't look beyond salary when it comes to negotiating. This happens at all levels of role and experience. Remember, there are multiple components of your offer that can be equally as important.

Negotiation Planning: Salary and Compensation

The following section includes things you should definitely, maybe, and minimally negotiate.

Definitely Negotiate: Salary, Stock, Sign-On, and Start Date
Your first step is data collection, which you should start by reaching out to people within that organization and people with

similar roles in other organizations. We also encourage you to tap into any school or alumni career resources. Find out the following from your network:

- their understanding of the salary for the role you are negotiating
- how the entire compensation package is structured
- if sign-on bonuses are typical and, if so, an estimate of the amount.

Get salary and other data from these sites: Comparably, Glassdoor, Salary.com, and LinkedIn. Each site gives you salary ranges for the role and also factors in location. Several also provide bonus amounts. Glassdoor also provides compensation for roles by companies, though the data is spotty when the company is small. LinkedIn often provides salary information if you have a premium account.

Data from Comparably, Glassdoor, and Salary.com is crowdsourced (provided anonymously by users). There is no checking or validation; keep that in mind as you review. Salary data from LinkedIn is usually listed in each job post and is provided directly by the company.

Write down the URL for the page with the job data. Even better, capture a screen shot; having both will be helpful. You'll need this information in this chapter's analysis exercise.

Maybe Negotiate: Relocation

Relocation amounts can vary a lot, especially in smaller companies. Larger companies often have set amounts and even relocation programs you can use. As we wrote about earlier, you want to get an understanding before the offer on how the company handles it.

If the company has a full program for relocation (moving services, relocation coordinators), then the only element you can discuss is the amount of money you will need. That amount can be negotiated, especially if you're relocating a partner/spouse and other family members.

Also consider negotiating if these situations are part of your relocation: (a) moving a long distance (we think of that as more than five hundred miles); (b) maintaining two homes for a period of time; (c) your partner or spouse may not be working.

Minimally Negotiate: Bonus and Commission

Bonuses are almost always company wide, with a defined evaluation structure and payment cycle. In almost all cases, bonuses aren't negotiable. A rare exception is if the company has a loosely structured plan with a lot of latitude. We haven't seen them often; usually they are in smaller or earlier-stage companies. This would be the only time you should consider negotiating.

Commissions, which are paid out to sales or business development staff, also usually have a structure and payment cycle. But there is a possible negotiation area: a commission ramp.

As we discussed earlier, some companies provide a full or partial commission in the first few months after starting, also known as ramp. Find out of the company offers a guarantee or ramp. If there's not a commission guarantee or ramp program, or if it's minimal, consider negotiating.

EXERCISE: THE OFFER AND THE RESEARCH

The table below captures the research you've done on the offer and sets you up for building your counteroffer. Getting data from friends and acquaintances can be helpful, but vet them carefully and use multiple sources. Unless they have actual data (not just second- or third-hand information or an opinion), don't use it.

We list multiple online sources in a few pages to help your research. Write out the details of the offer in each category. Note relevant data for each of the offer categories in the other columns.

Offer and research	Offer	Research source 1	Research source 2	Research source 3
Salary				
Bonus				
Stock/RUSs				
Sign-On				
Relocation				
Commission				

Receiving the Offer

This is where tone and self-control really come into play. You want to share appreciation for receiving the offer, but at all costs avoid the temptation to immediately start negotiating offer components.

But you do want to set a time line to respond. Things get tricky when you're involved with other companies, and especially if you're shortly expecting another offer. It's a terrific problem to have multiple offers, but managing the process can be challenging.

Setting the Time Line for the Counteroffer Discussion

The company is ready to sign you up, and you'll likely feel some pressure as they extend the offer. Now that you have the research model we just shared (and ideally, you've already begun), set a date to get back to them. The organization's ideal is for you to get back to them the next day. We recommend two to three business days, which looks like this:

Day offer extended	Reply by
Monday	Wednesday–Thursday (same week)
Tuesday	Thursday–Friday (same week)
Wednesday	Friday–Monday (runs over the weekend)
Thursday	Monday–Tuesday (of the next week)
Friday	Tuesday–Wednesday (of the next week)

There are exceptions. Some common ones are a significant work or personal commitment that is taking all your focus for more than two to three days, or expecting another offer or being in final-round interviews with another organization.

Unless the work or personal commitment is last minute, you should have let the company know up front you have a hectic schedule and might need more time to review an offer. The best time to do this is during the interview process.

Waiting for another offer or wanting to finish interviews with another company is trickier. It's much easier if you aim for transparency. As we discussed in the chapter on action plans, letting companies know you are in dialogue with others is important. Catherine, in this chapter's opening story, used that to her advantage.

But don't get carried away with the time line. As recruiters, we get really concerned if a candidate asks for an excessive period of time. We consider it excessive if a candidate asks for more than seven to ten working days (more than a week and a half) before a reply.

The company will be concerned with the candidate's real interest in the role. Do they genuinely want to join, or are they simply collecting offers? That is not the tone you want to set.

Salary and Compensation Questions and Considerations

There's a key value question you need clarity on: what you value more, salary (dollars) or equity (stock). This core value will drive your negotiation. This is not a judgment on greed; it's about understanding the ability and interest in taking more risk and less pay.

Both of us have worked in small companies and took more stock or equity in lieu of more salary. This didn't mean we weren't getting paid well. We were willing to take less salary and more equity because we felt the companies had promise and we wanted to support them. We hoped to be rewarded if the companies were acquired or went public.

Your current financial situation often dictates how you structure the mix. Mike joined a start-up while his son was in college. He structured his offer to take more salary than equity because of his financial commitments at that time.

After his son graduated, Mike took several leadership roles with more focus on equity. His life situation changed, and so did his ability to rebalance his salary versus equity approach.

If options or equity is offered, take it, but the question is how much. If your financial commitments are manageable and the company's future looks solid, then maybe adjust the offer to more stock than salary. This doesn't have to be a big ask, maybe a 10 percent adjustment between stock and salary.

Balancing your financial needs against taking more equity is a core decision, and making it *before* you start negotiating is key.

These are the elements of the offer you can and should negotiate. This is where good research pays off. Your key research should come from two areas: your existing business relationships or networks and online information.

Start Date

Surprisingly, start dates have been an area we've seen complicate offer negotiations. There are usually two reasons:

1. Prebooked vacations or other events: We've seen candidates avoid discussing this until negotiations, mostly out of fear they won't be considered. That rarely happens unless the time commitment is significant (a month or more).

2. A need to take a break before starting: Taking a break is natural and needed. The only time this is problematic is when the organization and the candidate have different start-date expectations.

These issues often come up when the candidate and recruiter haven't discussed the matter until the offer is presented. In most cases the company worked with the candidate to accommodate a later start date. But there are limits. If a candidate requested a start date more than a month out, then that was problematic. Usually, dates can be adjusted a bit on both sides to come up with a workable start date for all.

It's trickier if the start date is extended because the candidate is wrapping up other work at their previous job. Going beyond two to three weeks typically makes the new employer uncomfortable.

If there is a key project that you can't exit from, consider a part-time role with the new company. We call this a phase-in start date. If an employee can't start for five weeks because of a mission-critical project with their current company, think about offering to be part-time for a few weeks. This could even be phased in. Start part-time and adjust the weekly hours up if you can.

The best approach is letting the new employer know early. We've seen start dates disappoint new hiring managers when they found out during the offer negotiations. You don't want to start that relationship off in a bad light.

Job Title

We have seen the job title question slow down or even end a negotiation, especially if it is still an issue at the time of the offer. Both sides should reach agreement on the title *before* an offer is extended.

The biggest reason for this is how job titles affect compensation. If you are looking for a higher role, from a manager to a director, make sure this is locked down before you receive an offer.

In the scenario above, you want to be a director in the new company and are currently a manager. The company may counter with a senior manager title. You should explore the following:

- How does your experience match up with that of other senior managers in the organization? The same question should also be asked about the director's experience.

- What kind of growth path is there for a senior manager to move to a director? Understand what performance you'd need to demonstrate to be promoted. Also get clear on their promotion process and how frequently the organization does promote.

- When we face tough economic conditions, job titles in your career progression are not as important. As recruiters, we understand that during recessions and other economically challenging times, people often accept jobs more for economic reasons than they might normally. We recognize that working and keeping a steady income sometimes wins out over a job-title increase.

In fact, both we and other recruiters we know don't worry about the title as much—we focus more on the accomplishments, contributions, and career growth.

Your Counteroffer

As emphasized throughout this book, research is a strength. Now that you've got data, this exercise will help you to package it and get you ready to share your counteroffer.

First, you don't have to negotiate every component of the offer if those components are in line with your research. You want to focus your counteroffer on the components that are not in range.

Presenting a single number in a counteroffer is problematic. We *always* encourage our clients and students to come back with a range. The exercise for this instructs you to note a low number and a high number. Together they will become your range.

The low number should be slightly above your bottom line or "floor." The high number should be based on your research, not your emotions. It also depends on both the marketplace and the company's situation. Deepak Malhotra, Harvard professor and author of *Negotiating the Impossible: How to Break Deadlocks and Resolve Ugly Conflicts (without Money or Muscle)*, describes this as knowing the company's constraints.

Your job is to figure out where they're flexible and where they're not. If, for example, you're talking to a large company that's hiring 20 similar people at the same time, it probably can't give you a higher salary than everyone else. But it may be flexible on start dates, vacation time, and signing bonuses.

On the other hand, if you're negotiating with a smaller company that has never hired someone in your role, there may be room to adjust the initial salary offer or job title but not other things. The better you understand the constraints, the more likely it is that you'll be able to propose options that solve both sides' problems. (18)

EXERCISE: WRITE OUT YOUR COUNTEROFFER

Write out the offer in the first column and then the low number and high number for each of the areas. Note: this is to prepare you for discussing the ranges for each offer.

Do not send this table!

Counteroffer	Existing offer	Low number	High number
Salary			
Stock/RSUs			
Sign-on			

Relocation			

Counteroffers should be presented verbally. Even if that feels uncomfortable, it is the best way to avoid misunderstandings and confusion if a counter is sent in an email. This is the structure of a counteroffer:

- Open with a positive, collaborative statement.
- Tell them the offer components you've accepted.
- List the components you want to negotiate.
- Share the research you've done.
- Present a range for each offer component.
- Close with a strong affirming statement.

We'll go into each part in more detail below.

Open with a positive, collaborative statement. Let them know clearly that you are sincerely interested in the role and want to join the organization. The other statement to make is that you want to collaborate with the recruiter (or whoever is extending the offer) to reach agreement. If the offer is close, tell them that and point out that your desired numbers represent an "adjustment."

Tell them the offer components you've accepted. Up front, summarize the components of the offer you are ready to accept as is! Your enthusiastic response, along with your emphasis on collaboration and highlighting the acceptable elements of the offer, will start your dialogue with a positive tone, reduce pressure, and signal that an agreement is close.

List the components you want to negotiate. Presenting all the counteroffer components at one time is our strong recommendation. Malhotra also concurs:

> If you ask for only one thing initially, they may assume that getting it will make you ready to accept the offer (or at least to decide). If you keep saying "and one more thing . . . ," they are unlikely to remain in a generous or understanding mood. Furthermore, if you have more than one request, don't simply mention all the things you want—A, B, C, and D; also signal the relative importance of each to you. (18)

Share the research you've done. Provide an overview of the research you've done. Mention the sources you've used, such as the sites you've reviewed and the data you've collected. If you are sharing data from people, make sure they are credible and that their information is fact, not just opinion.

Present a range for each offer component. Presenting ranges allows you to identify a bottom line without having to disclose one, and you come across as flexible and open to negotiation.

Close with a strong affirming statement. You want to reiterate that this is a job you want and that the counteroffer you've shared is designed to be realistic for both sides. This will also set the tone for how well you'll work with your team going forward. Demonstrate competence by making sure both sides win. Establish goodwill with your new company.

Below is a sample counteroffer presentation where the stock component is acceptable, but both the salary and sign-on bonus are low.

> I want to again thank you for this offer and emphasize that I'm very interested in the role and the organization. I want to join, and I look forward to collaborating with you to make that happen.
>
> First let me share that the stock options are fine; they're right in the range.
>
> There are just two areas I want to propose adjustments to, the salary and sign-on bonus, based on research that I've done. I've talked with a person who has the same role in the same size company. Also, I've researched and have data from both LinkedIn and Comparably. Based on this market information, I want to see a salary between [the low number] and [the high number].
>
> The sign-on bonus is close. Based on the data, I'd like to look at a sign-on bonus in the range of [the low number] and [the high number].
>
> I wanted to give you ranges to help us reach an agreement. I'm serious about accepting a revised offer and becoming a high-contribution team member.
>
> What are the next steps?

> "This part is what I ignored before - lesson learned is that negotiation is almost a no-lose game. If you do not negotiate, you get what already is being offered; if you negotiate, you could possibly get more."
>
> **Tao Huang**

Other Counteroffer Considerations

Steve had a recent client whom he assisted in her offer negotiation. She had done two counteroffers and was considering a third one. Here is the email Steve sent her that perfectly explains the counteroffer process:

> In general, they make an offer, you counter, and then they come back with an offer that meets your requirements. Unless they are way off with the final offer, that should be it.
>
> When you start going back and forth too many times, this could impact the goodwill that's been established. So, I ask, is the 10K a deal breaker for you? If it's super important to you, then ask for it, because now is when you have the most leverage in the process. However, asking for increases at the very end of the negotiation is called nibbling. They already increased your sign-on once.
>
> If that additional 10K closes the final gap toward your target package, and they know this, then you can push. If to them, your request feels like it's coming out of left field, then you must ask yourself if this request is worth the tension it may cause.

In cases where the revised offer is still outside your range, Malhotra has sage advice:

> Sadly, to many people, "negotiating a job offer" and "negotiating a salary" are synonymous. But much of your satisfaction from the job will come from other factors you can negotiate—perhaps even more easily than salary.
>
> Don't get fixated on money. Focus on the value of the entire deal: responsibilities, location, travel, flexibility in work hours, opportunities for growth and promotion, perks, support for continued education, and so forth. Think not just about how you're willing to be rewarded but also when. You may decide to chart a course that pays less handsomely now but will put you in a stronger position later. (18)

A job offer is not just a series of numbers; it's the gateway to building skills and experiences that will create career value. Making strong, sensible counteroffers needs to be the norm for an entire working career.

But when all the factors are considered, including how the role matches up with your values and interests, don't walk away on just a number.

If they are off by a little, consider if it's worth it. As Steve asked his client, "Is the 10K a deal breaker for you?" She decided that it wasn't and accepted the new job.

An offer that is significantly under the range you proposed may make you feel discounted and could affect your motivation. Pay attention to this; it could be a concern.

But if the organization comes back and explains the rationale for the offer and it sounds legitimate, then it might be worth accepting. Especially if they're willing to adjust smaller elements for you.

Understanding Benefits

Too often benefits get little attention, or just a cursory glance. We frequently see clients simply look at who the health insurance provider is and maybe the cost. We strongly recommend taking time to understand the benefits package in more detail. We break down benefits into four categories:

- health and wellness
- time off or paid time off (PTO)
- retirement savings programs
- perks and expenses

We are highlighting the most common areas. This is meant to provide a framework in which to evaluate the benefits package, knowing that packages vary a great deal. Below is a breakdown of each area.

Health and Wellness

This category includes several subcategories, as noted below.

Medical, Dental, Vision, and Other

This is the core of a benefits package. You want to understand the following:

- Do they provide all of these or just core medical and dental?
- What type of health care plan is it, PPO or HMO?
- Is it a high-deductible plan? (A high-deductible plan is somewhat self-explanatory; you may pay a lower monthly premium but have a higher deductible, meaning you pay for more of your health care items and services before the insurance plan pays.)
- How soon after you start will benefits begin?
- What is the amount paid by the employer for you?
- What is the amount paid by the employer for a spouse and dependents?
- What out-of-pocket expenses will you have for office visits, prescriptions, specialists, dental annual coverage limits and percentages for cleaning and treatments, and vision annual coverage limits?

Each of the questions are centered on costs. How much are you paying each paycheck and for each medical or dental interaction?

Make sure you understand how the new health plan covers services that you, your partner/spouse, and your family will continue to use, including mental health services. What is the maximum coverage annually for these services, and what is your out-of-pocket amount for each interaction?

Focus on when your benefits start and how that meshes with your existing benefits. We've seen people become uncovered for a month or more when they didn't ask.

Here's an idea: if you do end up with a coverage gap period, and you must pay through COBRA to maintain coverage for a month, then that amount could become part of a sign-on bonus.

Health Savings Programs

The major programs that can be offered include health savings accounts or medical savings accounts (HSAs or MSAs), flexible spending arrangements (FSAs), and health reimbursement arrangements, or HRAs. (11) We won't get into too much detail, but these programs can be important benefits that are good ways to build up nontaxed medical savings.

An HSA or MSA is a type of savings account that lets you set aside money on a pretax basis to pay for qualified medical expenses. By using untaxed dollars in an HSA or MSA to pay for deductibles, copayments, coinsurance, and certain other expenses, you may be able to lower your overall health care costs. HSA and MSA funds generally may not be used to pay premiums.

An HSA is available if you have a high-deductible health plan (HDHP): generally a health plan (including a Marketplace plan) that only covers preventive services before the deductible. (12) An MSA is usually offered by a small company of fewer than fifty employees.

An HRA is an employee-funded health reimbursement account that can be used to pay deductibles and other health care expenses that insurance doesn't pick up. The key difference lies in portability. An HSA or MSA plan can be kept and owned by the employee, whereas an HRA and its balance can't move with the employee when they leave the company. (13)

FSAs can cover medical expenses up to a certain amount each year (in 2020 this amount was $2,750). They apply to copayments and deductibles. Often an employee is given an FSA debit card to use. One key point to remember is that it's a "use it or lose it" contribution. Contributions cannot be carried over year to year. (15)

Wellness Programs

Employers or their health care providers sometimes offer low- or no-cost wellness programs such as smoking cessation, weight loss, or getting-healthy programs. Check for these options in the benefits guide they provide you or simply ask about them.

We've seen employers include some benefits for chiropractic or acupuncture programs. If you use these services or want to use them, check on this.

PTO, Sick Leave, and Other Cases

Time off, also called paid time off or PTO, can have a lot of components. To simplify, below are three key questions to ask and understand:

QUESTION: "Is the PTO unlimited, or are set hours or days accrued each year?"

Answer: Unlimited PTO has been growing, so check whether this is in the policy.

QUESTION: "If not unlimited, how many hours or days are there in the PTO plan for year one and after the first year?"

Answer: Ten days is the average number of PTO for private-sector employees who have completed one year of service, according to the Bureau of Labor Statistics (BLS). This does not include sick days or paid holidays. But it turns out that the average PTO length varies substantially, depending on a number of factors, including tenure with a company, public versus private industries, and your geographic location. (16) Paid vacations were available to 76 percent of private-industry workers in March 2017. On average, workers received ten paid vacation days after one year of service. The number of paid vacation days increases slightly as tenure with the current employer increases. After five years, workers received fifteen paid days on average. They received an average of seventeen days after ten years and twenty days after twenty years. (17)

QUESTION: "Does the PTO include vacation and sick days?"

Answer: Note that the numbers cited above are vacation days only, not sick leave. Some PTO programs will bundle the vacation and sick days together. Make sure you completely understand this. Generally, you will see that a bundled PTO (vacation and sick days) program has more days.

Other key questions include the following:

QUESTION: "What is my accrual cycle for PTO?"

Answer: It is usually monthly or by paycheck period. Understand the amount you accrue for each cycle.

QUESTION: "When can I start using my PTO time?"

Answer: Some companies let employees immediately use PTO time; others have a window, often three or six months.

QUESTION: "How much of my PTO can I carry over from year to year? Is there a maximum number of PTO hours?"

Answer: We hope you use your PTO time each year. It's there for you to take time and live a balanced life. But if you don't use all your PTO time, make sure you know the limit of hours you can carry over. We've seen PTO plans with a limit on the number of PTO hours you can carry over each year. Additionally, PTO plans often set a maximum number of hours you can have. Once you reach the maximum, you cannot carry over any more hours.

The above assumes that the benefits don't bundle sick leave and vacation leave together in their PTO plan. Make sure you understand the answers to the following questions related to sick leave.

QUESTION: "What is the amount of days of sick leave?"

Answer: According to the Bureau of Labor Statistics:

> 71 percent of workers in private industry had paid sick leave benefits. About 6 in 10 of those workers received a fixed number of sick leave days each year. Four percent could use sick days as needed, and the rest were in consolidated leave plans, which provide time off for workers to use for a variety of purposes.
>
> Among those who received a fixed number of sick leave days, the amount varied depending on the employee's length of service and the size of the establishment.
>
> On average, workers in private industry received seven days of sick leave per year at one year of service. The average also was seven days at five and ten years of service and eight sick days per year at twenty years of

> service. Employees in smaller establishments received fewer paid sick days, on average, than employees in establishments with five hundred workers or more. (13)

QUESTION: "Can you carry over sick leave from year to year?"

Answer: Again, from the Bureau of Labor Statistics:

> In March 2018, 46 percent of workers in private industry who received a fixed number of paid sick days could carry over unused sick days from year to year. Usually there was a limit to the number of days these workers could carry over. The remaining 54 percent of workers in private industry could not carry over unused sick days from one year to the next. (13)

QUESTION: "What annual holidays does the company observe?"

Answer: Check the list of observed holidays. They can vary a lot and in some cases are regional. Also check to see if there are any floating holidays as well.

Retirement and Other Savings Programs

In most businesses that offer retirement programs such as IRAs (individual retirement accounts), you are offered a 401(k), a SIMPLE IRA (Savings Incentive Match Plan for Employees), or a SEP IRA (Simplified Employee Pension Plan). They are basically the same, but the size of the company, based on the number of employees, indicates which plan is used. Some organizations also offer Roth IRA programs.

Similar programs exist for nonprofits (403[b]) and for state and local governments (457[b]). (18). We won't go into detail on these except to recommend you find out the following.

QUESTION: "How much does the company contribute, and what is their vesting cycle?"

Answer: An average is around 6 percent, but we've seen smaller companies contribute anywhere from zero to amounts well over 6 percent. Along with this, look at how the vesting schedule for the company contribution works. Usually it is over two to four years.

Education Savings Programs

Education savings plans are investment accounts that enable you to save for qualified higher education expenses, including tuition, fees, and room and board. They can also be used for elementary or secondary school tuition (up to $10,000 a year).

Earnings from education savings plans are exempt from federal income taxes if distributions are used for qualified educational expenses. Many states also do not tax these earnings. (19)

Tuition Assistance

With this employee benefit, an employer pays for a predetermined amount of continuing education credits or college coursework to be applied toward a degree. These programs are intended for employees looking to advance their education. Typically, the coursework relates to their current career role or career track. The goal is to increase their industry knowledge and develop advanced skills.

If you plan to continue your education while working, be aware of this benefit. Surprisingly, many aren't aware of or utilizing it. A 2015 survey found that over 83 percent of organizations offered some type of tuition reimbursement benefit. On average, however, only 2 to 5 percent of eligible employees use tuition assistance programs, and 43 percent of working professionals are unaware of their employer's benefit. (20)

Perks and Expenses

Commuter benefits are a feature that only employers can offer. These perks allow employees to opt to have pretax money withheld from their paychecks to cover the cost of commuting. For 2020, the federal government allowed $270 per month to be withheld for commuting, and then an additional $270 a month for parking. (19)

Organizations often provide nice discounts on their own *products and services*; make sure you check on this perk. We've also seen companies offer discounts to employees that are provided by the company's suppliers. Often these discounts can be used by family and friends.

We see more and more organizations providing *laptops and computers* to new employees, especially for cybersecurity reasons. By providing their own laptops and computers, the organization can feel confident that the underlying setup and software will meet their security requirements. Ask whether the company is a "Mac shop" or a "PC place" or if you get a choice.

Find out about the policy on paying some of the cost of *phone service*; in California it's legally required. According to a 2018 survey, 89 percent of organizations provided a full or partial stipend to compensate BYOD ("Bring Your Own Device") employees for their mobile phone expenses. Businesses and organizations that provide mobile phone stipends for BYOD employees paid $36.13 per month on average, according to the survey. This amounts to about $430 per year for each employee. (21) Find out if the program exists, how much you receive, and if there is any documentation you need to provide. Often, it's just automatically included in your paycheck.

Finally, some organizations include stipends for having a *home office*, so check on this.

Summary

Entering negotiations with a structure and models should give you more confidence and more power. Though it may seem like a lot of content, we've seen many of our clients build on each successful job negotiation and get better and better at it.

- Know the compensation data before you start negotiating.
- Know the structure of the organization's offers early in the hiring process.
- Your first dialog about compensation is NOT a discussion. It is a leveling exercise to make sure both sides are in the same range.
- Break down your counter in pieces and think of them as levers.
- Understand what compensation elements are easy to negotiate and those that aren't.
- Watch out for shiny objects: be clear about how the company and the offer tie into your personal and career values and aspirations.
- Set a collaborative tone with the recruiter or negotiator. It will help get the right deal done and set the right tone with leadership.
- Indicate your interest as part of setting the tone.
- Agree to timelines for decisions on both sides.
- Clarify the start date and disclose any existing vacation or travel planning.

FINAL THOUGHTS AND ENCOURAGEMENT

We are pleased you've made it this far! By working through the exercises and chapters in this book, you will be stronger at your job search now and for the rest of your career.

That is an audacious statement, but it is validated by the many success stories of our clients at all points in their careers. Job searching should not be feared, and it should not be so intimidating that people stay in roles that make them miserable. Giving people knowledge and freedom to grow, change, and improve their careers is our passion and mission.

We are committed to making job searching a skill. When you treat it as a skill, you will work toward improving the steps and enhancing the processes every time you make a change.

You will also focus on building strong relationships that will benefit both parties throughout your career and beyond. These relationships are a key win in your career and a source of ideas and strength.

We will continue to grow and deepen The Job Search Manifesto. Things are constantly changing, and how we move into a post-pandemic world has great implications for work and careers. Our vantage point is unique, and we'll use it to keep you updated and informed. Look for updated content on our website, jobsearchmanifesto.com, along with updates to this book.

We wish you success in your career and hope to be a continued resource for growing and developing yourself, and your career.

Notes

1. Just how long do employees stay at Uber, Dropbox and Salesforce? . *San Francisco Business Journal.* [Online] April 10, 2017. https://www.bizjournals.com/sanfrancisco/news/2018/04/10/employee-retention-big-bay-area-tech-companies.html.

2. Alison Doyle. Steps in the Interview Process. *The Balance Careers.* [Online] January 4, 2020. https://www.thebalancecareers.com/steps-in-the-job-interview-process-2061363.

3. Dictionary.com/manifesto. *Dictionary.com.* [Online] https://www.dictionary.com/browse/manifesto.

4. Digital Agency Network. How To Create Personas For Marketing In 2020. *Digital Agency Network.* [Online] https://digitalagencynetwork.com/how-to-create-personas-for-marketing/.

5. Anna Ranieri. hrb.org. *Harvard Business Review.* [Online] August 15, 2015. [Cited: March 29, 2020.] https://hbr.org/2015/08/turning-your-complex-career-path-into-a-coherent-story.

6. Csikszentmihalyi, Mihaly. *Finding Flow: The Psychology of Engagement with Everyday Life.* 1997.

7. Paul Petrone. The Skills Companies Need Most in 2018 – And The Courses to Get Them. *LinkedIn Learning.* [Online] January 2, 2018. https://learning.linkedin.com/blog/top-skills/the-skills-companies-need-most-in-2018--and-the-courses-to-get-t.

8. Graham, Dr. Dawn. *Switchers.* s.l. : AMACOM, 2018.

9. Burkus, David. *Friend of a Friend Friend of a Friend . . .: Understanding the Hidden Networks That Can Transform Your Life and Your Career .*

10. Matthews, Kayla. 13 Email Marketing Statistics That Are Shaping 2019 and Beyond. *Convince and Convert.* [Online] 2019. https://www.convinceandconvert.com/digital-marketing/email-marketing-statistics/.

11. Career Contessa. Subject Lines That Will Get Your Cold Email Noticed. *Careercontessa.com.* [Online] August 4, 2020. https://www.careercontessa.com/advice/cold-email-subject-lines/.

12. LinkedIn. The Recruiter's Guide to writing effective LinkedIn InMails. [Online] https://business.linkedin.com/content/dam/business/talent-solutions/global/en_US/c/pdfs/the-recruiters-guide-to-writing-effective-linkedin-inmails.pdf.

13. Mailchimp. Average email marketing campaign stats of Mailchimp customers by industry. *Mailchimp.com.* [Online] 2018. https://mailchimp.com/resources/email-marketing-benchmarks/.

14. Melissa Darcey. FMGSuite. *fmgsuite.com.* [Online] February 5, 2016. https://fmgsuite.com/market-in-motion/magnet-or-megaphone/.

15. Paycor.com. States With Salary History Bans. *Paycor.com.* [Online] December 8, 2020. https://www.paycor.com/resource-center/states-with-salary-history-bans.

16. Adler, Lou. *Hiring with Your Head: Using Performance-Based Hiring to Build Great Teams, Third Edition.* s.l. : John Wiley and Sons, 2007.

17. Katie Shonk. How to Negotiate Salary: 3 Winning Strategies - PON - Program on Negotiation at Harvard Law School. *Program on Negotation, Harvard Law School.* [Online] October 29, 2019. https://www.pon.harvard.edu/daily/salary-negotiations/negotiate-salary-3-winning-strategies/.

18. Grant, Adam. In Negotiations, Givers Are Smarter Than Takers. *New York Times.* [Online] March 27, 2020. [Cited: April 4, 2020.] https://www.nytimes.com/2020/03/27/smarter-living/negotiation-tips-giver-taker.html.

19. Deepak Malhotra. 15 Rules for Negotiating a Job Offer. *Harvard Business Review.* [Online] April 2014. https://hbr.org/2014/04/15-rules-for-negotiating-a-job-offer.

20. FSA Store. What is a flexible spending account? *FSA Store.* [Online] https://fsastore.com/what-is-an-FSA.

21. Jean Spencer. How Much Is Average for PTO? *Workest powered by Zenefits.* [Online] October 23, 2018. https://www.zenefits.com/workest/how-much-is-average-pto-in-the-us/.

22. Bureau of Labor Statistics. Private industry workers received average of 15 paid vacation days after 5 years of service in 2017. *TED: The Economics Daily.* [Online] https://www.bls.gov/opub/ted/2018/private-industry-workers-received-average-of-15-paid-vacation-days-after-5-years-of-service-in-2017.htm.

23. Rachel Hartman. Retirement Accounts You Should Consider. *US News and World Reports.* [Online] December 18, 2019. https://money.usnews.com/money/retirement/articles/retirement-accounts-you-should-consider.

24. Matt Mansfield. What's a 529 Plan? Can I Offer a 529 Plan as an Employee Benefit? *Gusto.* [Online] https://gusto.com/blog/benefits/529-college-savings-plan.

25. Tracy Scott. TUITION REIMBURSEMENT PROGRAMS: WHY AND HOW TO TAKE ADVANTAGE OF YOUR EMPLOYEE BENEFIT. *Northeastern University Graduate Programs.* [Online] December 3, 2018. https://www.northeastern.edu/graduate/blog/tuition-reimbursement/.

26. Samsung for Business. How Much Should You Compensate BYOD Employees for Mobile Expenses? *Samsung.com.* [Online] https://insights.samsung.com/2020/02/04/how-much-should-you-compensate-byod-employees-for-mobile-expenses-2/.

27. Bruce Anderson. LinkedIn's Head of Recruiting Shares His Tips for Setting Realistic Hiring Timelines. *LinkedIn Talent Blog.* [Online] February 28, 2019. https://business.linkedin.com/talent-solutions/blog/talent-on-tap/2019/linkedins-head-of-recruiting-tips-for-setting-realistic-hiring-timelines.

28. Mike Manoske. The Smart Job Candidate: Know the Hiring Process. *MikeCoach.com.* [Online] March 10, 2019. http://www.mikecoach.com/post/2019/03/13/the-smart-job-candidate-know-the-hiring-process.

29. Aine Cain. BusinessInsider.com. *Business Insider.* [Online] December 30, 2019. https://www.businessinsider.com/the-perfect-email-subject-line-for-job-hunting-2014-3.

30. Shana Lebowitz. BusinessInsider.com. *Business Insider.* [Online] February 1, 2017. https://www.businessinsider.com/best-way-to-end-an-email-2017-2.

31. Indeed.com. Hard Skills vs. Soft Skills. *Indeed.com.* [Online] January 26, 2020. https://www.indeed.com/career-advice/resumes-cover-letters/hard-skills-vs-soft-skills.

32. Internal Revenue Service. Publication 969 (2019), Health Savings Accounts and Other Tax-Favored Health Plans. *IRS.gov.* [Online] 2019. https://www.irs.gov/publications/p969.

33. Healthcare.gov. Health Savings Account (HSA). *Healthcare.gov.* [Online] https://www.healthcare.gov/glossary/health-savings-account-hsa/.

34. Datapath. HRA vs HSA – What's the Difference? *Datapath.* [Online] https://dpath.com/hra-vs-hsa-whats-the-difference/.

35. 12 Answers to Common 'Paid Time Off' Questions. *ERC.* [Online] https://www.yourerc.com/blog/post/12-answers-to-common-paid-time-off-questions.

36. Bureau of Labor Statistics. Private industry workers with sick leave benefits received 8 days per year at 20 years of service. *TED: The Economics Daily image.* [Online] March 8, 2019. https://www.bls.gov/opub/ted/2019/private-industry-workers-with-sick-leave-benefits-received-8-days-per-year-at-20-years-of-service.htm.

37. Justworks. It's About Time to Offer Your Employees Commuter Benefits. *Justworks.* [Online] October 23, 2018. https://justworks.com/blog/offer-your-employees-commuter-benefits-everyone-saves-money.

38. Grant, Adam. The science of the deal. *WorkLife with Adam Grant Podcast.* [Online] March 2020. https://www.ted.com/talks/worklife_with_adam_grant_the_science_of_the_deal.

39. Clear, James. Core Values List. *JamesClear.com.* [Online] https://jamesclear.com/core-values.

40. Companies with the least and most loyal employees - The Least Loyal Employees. *Payscale.com.* [Online] https://www.payscale.com/data-packages/employee-loyalty/least-loyal-employees.

41. Employee Tenure in 2018. *United States Department of Labor, Bureau of Labor Statistics.* [Online] September 2018. https://www.bls.gov/news.release/pdf/tenure.pdf.

Glossary

Accomplishment—a specific project or task you've completed that demonstrates your abilities.

Applicant tracking system (ATS)—a piece of software that sorts through application candidates. Recruiters frequently use ATSs to narrow applications they've received through job boards.

Contingent recruiter—An external recruiter who is always searching for the next position to fill using a transactional numbers game. Candidates will only get feedback from them if they are qualified for the position the recruiter is trying to fill. Contingent recruiters may or may not have in-depth information about the role, company, or leadership team. They typically receive 20 percent of the candidate's annual salary.

Corporation—a business that is legally separate from its owners. While all corporations are companies, not all companies are corporations.

Culture fit—how much an employee's attitudes, beliefs, and behaviors align with the company's values and how well the employee can adapt to the company's work environment.

Dormant ties—strong or weak ties (see below) you have lost contact with. Usually, you can reconnect with them easily, as if it'd only been a few days since the last time you saw them.

Elevator pitch—a short description of a person, company, or idea delivered succinctly in a short period of time; an advertisement delivered verbally from one person to another.

Executive recruiter—retained recruiters with a focus on senior leadership positions. Their initial payment and their percentage on the back end are higher than those of other retained recruiters. They will sometimes receive options, and they are the most detailed of all recruiters in their screening and candidate preparation. Usually they are focused on VP to C-level roles. They are often the most experienced recruiters, and some can give you good information about industries.

Experience—something you've done well multiple times throughout your career; an experience is more cumulative than an accomplishment.

External recruiter—an individual or recruiting agency that works on behalf of a company to fill one or more positions.

Fortune 100 company—a company that *Fortune* magazine has listed as one of the top one hundred companies in the United States.

Hiring manager—the person who is looking for a new employee to fill a position.

HSA—health savings account.

Industry—a group of companies that produce a similar good or service.

InMail—LinkedIn's messaging service for premium accounts.

Internal/corporate recruiter—internal recruiters, also known as corporate recruiters, are employees of the companies they work for. They have a better understanding of the role in the company than an external recruiter would, and they are directly involved with the hiring process. Unfortunately, they usually have a lot on their plates, so it may be difficult for them to find time to give you the feedback you need.

IPO—initial public offering: a company's first time selling shares on the stock market; an independent, publicly owned company.

Job board—a website where companies can post job openings; people can often submit applications through the website as well.

Proactive job search—a job search in which someone looks for work through techniques such as targeting specific employers and/or companies and utilizing contacts to obtain advice and/or referrals.

PTO—paid time off.

Reactive job search—a job search in which someone looks for work primarily through job boards or by waiting for a recruiter to reach out; this approach is often ineffective.

Retained recruiter—a more experienced recruiter who generally works with filling senior positions. Retained recruiters usually receive an initial payment up front with a percentage bonus when a candidate accepts an offer. Because retained recruiters have a more stable cash flow than most other kinds of recruiters, they can spend extra time on their search. For a candidate, this means they are more likely to provide feedback and in-depth information about the role they're trying to fill.

RSU—restricted stock unit; company stocks issued to employees as payment.

SAR model—SAR stands for "situation, action, and result." The traditional way to model a résumé is by using STAR: situation, tactics, action, and results. In *The Job Search Manifesto*, we recommend you wait until the interview to explain "tactics." Including it in a résumé adds too much detail.

Strong ties—relationships with a strong trust base in which both parties are motivated to help each other. In a job search, these are the people we tend to go to first.

Weak ties—people you have a polite, friendly, but not deep relationship with. Though they may not seem valuable at first, they can provide new insights and act as a bridge between different groups.

LinkedIn Profile and Résumé Wording

Action Words and Phrases to Use:

Technical / organizational	Creative	Social
Analyzed	Authored	Administered
Arranged	Built	Advertised
Assessed	Composed	Advised
Audited	Conceptualized	Arbitrated
Broadened	Created	Assisted
Budgeted	Customized	Coached
Calculated	Defined	Collaborated
Catalogued	Designed	Consulted
Charted	Developed	Convinced
Coded	Established	Coordinated
Collected	Fashioned	Corresponded
Combined	Formed	Counseled
Compiled	Formulated	Delivered
Computed	Founded	Discussed
Corrected	Generated	Distributed

Technical / organizational	Creative	Social
Documented	Illustrated	Educated
Earned	Instituted	Explained
Edited	Invented	Guided
Enhanced	Originated	Influenced
Evaluated	Shaped	Instructed
Executed	Transformed	Interviewed
Identified	Wrote	Lectured
Implemented		Led
Improved		Managed
Increased		Negotiated
Interpreted		Orchestrated
Launched		Oversaw
Maintained		Participated
Marketed		Persuaded
Maximized		Promoted
Measured		Recruited
Merged		Referred
Minimized		Reported
Monitored		Reviewed
Navigated		Served
Organized		Solicited
Overhauled		Spoke
Planned		Surveyed

Technical / organizational	Creative	Social
Prepared		Trained
Programmed		
Purchased		
Reinforced		
Repaired		
Researched		
Reviewed		
Scheduled		
Sold		
Solved		
Standardized		
Streamlined		
Strengthened		
Structured		
Supplied		
Surpassed		
Synthesized		
Systematized		
Tested		
Translated		
Updated		
Utilized		
Verified		
Won		

Words and Phrases to Avoid :

Accomplished
Ambitious
Best of breed
Can't
Creative
Customer-centric
Dabbled
Detail-oriented
Dynamic
Excellent communicator
Familiar with
Fast learner
Game changer
Going forward
Go-to person
Hard worker / hardworking
Highly qualified
Hit the ground running
Hustle
I feel
Influencer
Leadership
Learning
Microsoft Office
Paradigm shift
People person
Phone and/or email
Proactive
References upon request
Results-driven / results-oriented
Reliable
Responsible for
Salary negotiable
Synergy
Team player
Think outside the box
Track Record
Won't

ACKNOWLEDGEMENTS

This book would never have been started or completed without the Job Search Action Group students at Wharton's Executive MBA Program in San Francisco. Attending sessions at 7:30 a.m. on Saturday mornings and evening sessions inspired us to share our best ideas and practices for your career.

We also thank the team who organized our ideas into this book, including researcher Jackie Caldwell; the Kirkus editorial team, headed by Heather Rodino; and the amazing book designer Yayun Chang-Cahill.

Steve's Acknowledgments

I'd first and foremost like to thank Mike Manoske for his leadership, friendship, and partnership in developing the Job Search Manifesto, and helping to elevate our Job Search Action Group program to a world-class level.

Thanks to my Wharton colleague Dr. Dawn Graham for her commitment to excellence, thoughtfulness, and always pushing me to think deeper.

Thanks to Bernie Birt, the best boss I've ever had, for her kindness, support, and unmatched ethics.

Thanks to my former business partner and lifelong friend Michael Inserra for his tutelage.

And finally thanks to my wife Vivian and son Chris for modeling what truth and honesty actually look like.

Mike's Acknowledgments

None of this would have happened without the passion, energy, and friendship of Steve Hernandez. I'm so honored to be his partner in JSAG, this book, and many future adventures. Thanks for inviting me in!

My clients teach me how to be a better coach. They, along with the students in the HireClub Bootcamps and the Mastermind Group, are on every page of this book. Ketan Anjaria, the founder of HireClub, Lisa Maria and Thao Pham have been great partners and teammates.

The recruiting teams at GoGrid (Shirley Vergara and Jeryn Blossom), Manage (including Ellie Jurchisin and Zona Pan) and Pebble (Jasmine Llacer Johnson, Ashley Donsky Johansen, Olivia Milhailova, Tania Monroe, Lisa Choi Oliver and Jeff Hyman) helped me grow as a leader. The Hudson Coaching Community, the Oasis Team led by Sandy Smith and the Hudson Book Club also are cornerstones in my coaching growth.

Special people worked with me several times; I'm grateful to Shirley Vergara, Kira Watkins-Kojerte, Tania Monroe, Jenna Wood, and Dan Miller.

Finally, to my wife, Antonette, and my son Andy: you are my North Stars.

About the Authors

Steve Hernandez

Steve brings 20 years of professional career development experience with the last ten years at the Wharton MBA for Executives program in San Francisco. At Wharton, Steve directs all areas of career advancement services including one-on-one coaching, career development programming, and partnership with the Wharton alumni community.

Prior to Wharton, Steve was an adjunct career advisor for the UC Berkeley Haas MBA programs. Before then Steve was a partner and executive recruiter for a local search firm where he helped Bay Area companies identify, screen, and hire professionals ranging from staff to senior management in a variety of industries, including banking, software, technology manufacturing, financial services, retail, consumer goods, biotechnology, and nonprofit.

In partnering with C-level executives, senior and middle managers, as well as human resources, Steve gained in-depth knowledge of the skills, communication, leadership, and behavioral traits that lead to success within organizations. Steve holds a master's degree in Career Development from John F. Kennedy University.

Mike Manoske

A Career Coach for more than a decade, Mike was also a Recruiter and Talent Acquisition Leader in Silicon Valley, hiring more than 1,000 people in engineering, sales, and marketing, finance, and operations.

Mike coaches and assists Steve in the Career Success programs at the Wharton Executive MBA Program in San Francisco. He is also the Director of Coaching for HireClub.com a Job and Career Community

A graduate of the Hudson Institute of Coaching, a Professional Certified Coach with the International Coaching Federation, Mike has a B.S. in Health Information Systems from Seattle University.

Visit our Website: Jobsearchmanifesto.com
For more the latest ideas and information, giveaways and special offers.

CPSIA information can be obtained
at www.ICGtesting.com
Printed in the USA
LVHW010626131021
700314LV00008B/419